I Love your new stor
over coffee and treats
WHAT DO STILL NEED TO DO?
Super Doop
so shiny
are to
I dont wa
Guest Check No.   Server
293765
105GCKDUP1CL
tines day 2020
7 years to the day
EMPTY
My Soul, My B
gels, The Holy Bread
OUR Bagel of Guadalupe
that had
BERN BA
LO
Abby
and
Bernha
From: James
Merlin WUZ HERE
CRAB IN
AF269418

BERN**B**AUM'S

SHALOM

RECIPES FROM FARGO'S NORDIC-JEWISH DELI

2016–2024

ANDREA BAUMGARDNER

Published in 2025 by Dottir Press
New York, NY

dottirpress.com

Second printing December 2025

Design and production: Drew Stevens
Editor: Jessica Baumgardner

Library of Congress Cataloging-in-Publication Data is available for this title.

ISBN 978-1-948340-63-2

Manufactured in India by Manipal Technologies Limited.

Contents

Introduction

What is this BernBaum's, the restaurant behind the cookbook you hold in your hands? Our shorthand was always that BernBaum's is a Nordic–Jewish deli, even though a few felt it necessary to let us know *that isn't a thing*.

Possibly true . . . until nine years ago in Fargo, North Dakota. I had been a chef and restaurant owner for over twenty years, but when I hit my late forties, I realized I needed a venture that would mesh better with my life: more time with my young son, Avi, and a respectably early bedtime. My husband, Brett, had made a good bagel at our last restaurant, Green Market, so we thought about a breakfast and lunch place. I specifically thought of B&H Dairy in the East Village in New York City—a tiny kosher lunch counter that serves soup, challah, and blintzes to however many can squeeze inside. Brett had extra room in the front of his midcentury furnishings store downtown, so we added seventeen seats and a small counter, plus a vintage electric stove from a friend's basement.

For our menu, we started with bagels from Brett's Jewish background and added in foods from my Icelandic and German roots. Oddly, there was overlap in the Venn diagram of these different cultures: a love of pickles, smoked fish and meats, rye, potatoes, cultured cream. We threw in a bit of Middle Eastern food because hummus is delicious and naturally vegan.

Monica McCoy in the bakery.

We opened March 9, 2016, expecting that we would see a few friends throughout the day. At noon, we had a rush of maybe twenty supporters (which felt like a hundred) and the whole operation almost ground to a halt. It was a teeny space, and I remember Brett issuing a blanket apology for our foolishness to the waiting crowd. Luckily our customers were patient, and over time we learned to anticipate a crowd. Amy Rice, a friend and fellow parent at Avi's school, was willing to work 9 to 2 five days a week, and BernBaum's survived. I am not resorting to hyperbole when I say that Amy had more to do with our success than anything else, but once we saw that Fargoans did want to eat bagels (and that Nordic–Jewish delis *were* a thing!), we started looking for a real kitchen.

We found one on Broadway, a strip of downtown Fargo that had been dead during my 1980s childhood but rebuilt by visionary small-business owners like Greg and Renee Danz of Zandbroz, Annele and Juan Mondragon of Juano's, and Karen Stoker of the Hotel Donaldson, to name just a few pioneers. We remodeled 402 Broadway, part of the historic Powers Hotel where Peggy Lee had sung in the 1930s, removing decades of forgotten equipment and the funk that accumulates in a century-old space. We now had a commercial kitchen, but one with many quirks—a rainbow of mismatched ceramic tile walls and battered stainless in lieu of gleaming flat surfaces and new pots. But several years in, the twenty or so of us who worked there (including my retired physician father, who made the bagel chips, flax crackers, and chili) filled it with fresh ingredients, talent, and real heart on a daily basis.

Regulars are essential to any small business, so although we were flattered to garner coverage in national media, like the *New York Times* and *Food & Wine*, the most meaningful reviews were handwritten notes stuffed into the vintage toy stoves adorning our south wall.

Our beloved customers often asked about a BernBaum's cookbook and I'd been working on one at a snail's pace due to my responsibilities at the restaurant. When we closed BernBaum's in the fall of 2024, surprising ourselves as much as our regulars, the concept of the cookbook as an archive—a record of a time, place, and its cast of characters—took hold. This is a snapshot of a small restaurant in a small city in the Midwest, both ordinary and original, thanks to our community within the restaurant and without.

I am an avid collector and reader of cookbooks, particularly ones that give the reader a sense of place and time and people. That is my ambition for this book. I hope that it is interesting because of where we are and the people who contributed to it, whether in spirit—like our grandmas, whose recipes we have adapted—or with their blood, sweat, and tears. The recipes included are the primer for BernBaum's, our deli fundamentals.

I'll end with some wisdom from our parents. After a death, Brett's mother, Bonnie, invokes the traditional Jewish "May their memory be a blessing," which I've always found comforting.

A Nordic–Jewish deli did exist. May its memory be a blessing.

Bagels, Breads, Knishes, and Crackers

Bread is the foundation of BernBaum's and it all starts with our bagels. When I first sat down to write this chapter, I left out our bagel recipe because I thought its multistep process would be off-putting to even a dedicated home baker. But my sisters reminded me that there is no BernBaum's without bagels, so this book starts with the bagel—or more accurately, the sourdough starter—and just as with the restaurant, the bagel is the foundation for all that came after it.

Sourdough Starter

To make some of these breads—and most importantly the bagels—you will need an active and well-cared-for sourdough starter. At its simplest, sourdough starter is a living culture of wild yeast and good bacteria that is regularly fed a diet of flour and water to keep it alive. This culture adds complex flavor, leavening, and keeping properties to bread. We created our starter using the recipe from *Nancy Silverton's Breads from the La Brea Bakery: Recipes for the Connoisseur*, a long title for a classic book that expertly describes the process.

If you don't want to make your own starter, I recommend getting a little from a friend, a local restaurant or bakery, or even online. We happily shared ours with anyone who asked. You still will have to maintain the starter once you have it, but at least you won't have to go through the two-week process of creating your own.

We used our sourdough starter daily for both bagels and rye bread, and fed it twice a day, morning and afternoon. But if you don't want to feed it daily, you can usually let your starter go dormant in the refrigerator for up to two weeks. Two days before you need it, start feeding it again. Between feedings, if we had more starter than we would need, we drained off the excess to use for pancakes and other projects.

STARTER FROM SCRATCH, THE HARD WAY (FOR MASOCHISTS)
Although there are shorter versions of creating a starter, this is the one I have used reliably. Buy yourself at least a 10-pound bag of unbleached bread flour to get through the next 2 weeks of feeding your starter.

Makes 2 cups (16 ounces) starter

> 18-inch square of cheesecloth, double-layered
>
> 1 pound organic grapes, washed
>
> 4 cups (32 ounces) lukewarm water
>
> 3¾ cups (19 ounces) unbleached bread flour

DAY 1: Place the double layer of cheesecloth on a clean work surface. Lay the grapes inside and tie the corners together to form a bag. Set aside.

In a 4-quart bowl, glass, or plastic container, add the water. Whisk in the flour until fully combined.

recipe continues

Hold the bag of grapes over the container and lightly squeeze with your free hand, mixing in the juice, then drop the whole bundle into the mixture.

Cover with a lid or piece of plastic wrap secured tightly around the rim. Keep at room temperature, 70° to 75°F.

DAYS 2 AND 3: Once each day, check your culture. The mixture will start to ferment and create bubbles of varying size and emit a yeasty and slightly sweet smell. Cover and allow it to continue fermenting at room temperature until day 4.

DAY 4: FEED THE STARTER

> 1 cup (8 ounces) lukewarm water
> 1 cup (5 ounces) unbleached bread flour

Remove the grapes from the culture and set aside. Pour in the water and whisk in the flour.

Put the grapes back into the culture and swish them through the mixture. Cover the container and let it continue to ferment for 5 days.

DAYS 5 THROUGH 9: Check your culture once each day. It is normal for the culture to separate. If mold appears, skim to remove the mold and feed the culture as on day 4.

DAY 10: Remove the bag of grapes, squeeze any liquid into the culture, and discard. Stir the starter and pour 2 cups into a clean 1-quart bowl or plastic container. Discard the rest. The remaining starter should be "active," with bubbles and a yeasty smell. If so, it is now ready for twice-a-day feedings to strengthen it.

> 2 cups (16 ounces) starter
> 1 cup (8 ounces) lukewarm water
> 1¼ cup (6.25 ounces) unbleached bread flour

Add the water and flour to the starter. Whisk or stir to mix well. Cover and let sit at room temperature.

Eight to twelve hours later, repeat.

The next morning, measure 2 cups of starter and feed as above. Repeat for 5 days.

MAINTAINING THE STARTER

Once the starter is mature and ready to use, continue with the twice-daily feedings or let it go dormant in the refrigerator (for up to 2 weeks) between baking projects.

> 1 cup (8 ounces) active sourdough starter
>
> ½ cup (4 ounces) water, body temperature*
>
> ½ cup + 2 tablespoons (3.2 ounces) unbleached bread flour
>
> *95° to 100°F; you can't feel a temperature change when you stick your finger in it.*

Using a Danish dough whisk or your gloved hands, mix the water and flour into the starter. Make sure that there are no lumps of dry flour. You will be able to use the starter 2 to 4 hours after feeding it. One way to check that your starter is ready is to drop a teaspoonful into a cup of cold water. If it floats, it's ready.

If you've made it this far, the rest of the book is a breeze, I promise. (Or at least it will be once you get past the breads!)

Bagels

At BernBaum's, we started the bagel–making process 24 hours before we planned to bake them. Each day by about 6:30 a.m., we fed the starter, which had last been fed the previous afternoon and rested in the cooler. Between 8:30 and 9:00 a.m., we mixed the dough, then let it proof (rise) for 2 to 3 hours. When the first proof was done, we cut and shaped the bagels, let them proof, then refrigerated them until the next morning. (This ensured a slower rise and thus more flavorful dough.) We boiled and baked that batch of bagels at around 6:00 the next morning.

As I've said, bagels were a linchpin of BernBaum's. But the other linchpin was Brett. Not only did he make the best bagels (although he practiced the least), he did the books and was the person on staff who could rebuild a small motor, fix leaky sinks, and plumb toilets. Never open a restaurant without a good bookkeeper and mechanic.

Remember to feed your starter 2 to 4 hours before you begin the recipe. Measure out what you need for this recipe and store the rest. This recipe extends over 2 days.

If you like, you can turn a few bagels out of the batch into Chagels (page 23) using 2 tablespoons of chocolate chips and a pinch of flaky sea salt per bagel. Or top some with Everything Bagel Mix (page 22).

As with all breads, times for mixing, proofing, and baking can vary depending on the temperature of the room, humidity, and even the specific character of your ingredients. With practice, you will learn what the starter looks like when active and how the dough looks and feels at each step.

Makes eight 4-ounce bagels. This recipe can be doubled or tripled.

- ¾ cup + 2 tablespoons (7 ounces) water, body temperature*
- ¾ teaspoon active dry yeast
- 1 tablespoon malt syrup**
- ¾ cup (6 ounces) active Sourdough Starter (page 11)
- 3 cups + 2 tablespoons (1 pound) unbleached bread flour,** (13% or higher protein content), plus more for flouring
- 1½ teaspoons Diamond Crystal kosher salt or ¾ teaspoon other kosher salt
- 2¼ teaspoons granulated sugar
- 2 tablespoons semolina or all-purpose flour, for dusting
- Unsalted butter, neutral oil, or nonstick baking spray, for greasing

**95 to 100°F; you can't feel a temperature change when you stick your finger in it.*
***Available at most grocery stores; check the natural food section.*

The hardest part of this recipe is the kneading. Kneading by hand will give you a workout, but it's worth it for good bread. At work, we used commercial mixers with bowls I could barely lift. I recommend using a home mixer only if (1) it is at least a 6–quart heavy–duty mixer with a dough hook, (2) you mix the dough in batches if you're doubling or tripling the recipe, and (3) you use the lowest speed. I burned out the motors of two home mixers trying to mechanize the process, so make sure you are not overloading your bowl—it should only be one-third full.

recipe continues

MIXING AND KNEADING BY HAND: Combine the water and yeast in a large bowl and whisk together until the yeast has dissolved. Add the malt syrup and starter and whisk to completely mix.

In a separate bowl, combine all but ¼ cup of bread flour, the salt, and the sugar. Stir this into the water-starter mixture. (If it is like North Dakota in the winter—very cold and dry—you will not need all of the flour.) Add the remaining ¼ cup of bread flour if the dough is wet and tacky when mixing.

As the flour combines with the wet ingredients, the dough will become harder to stir, so it is better to switch to using your hands. Flour your hands and continue to mix in the bowl until it becomes a uniform blob of dough, neither wet nor dry **1**. Cover with a clean kitchen towel and let sit for 20 minutes to let the dough relax before you knead.

Lightly flour a clean work surface (I like to use a wooden butcher block) and place the dough on it. Use one hand to pull out the far end of the dough and fold it over toward yourself onto the near end. Press it down using the heel of your hand **2**. The dough should be an oval shape. With your other hand, grab one side of the dough, stretch it, and fold it over the other side **3**.

Alternating hands, continue these folding motions for at least 12 minutes, more likely closer to 20. (This is a long time, so feel free to take breaks or share the work with a partner.) You can be vigorous with this dough, even slapping it on the table as you fold it over **4**. The dough will be ready when it is smooth like a baby's bottom and no longer tacky when you stick your finger into it **5**.

When it's ready, place it in a clean large bowl, cover the bowl with plastic wrap or a clean, damp flour sack towel and set aside at room temperature to ferment (that is, to rise before shaping).

> *Another way to check if the dough is kneaded enough is the windowpane test: Tear off a small piece of dough. Hold it in both hands between your thumbs and first two fingers, and gently stretch it to form a rectangle. If it can stretch to a thin membrane without breaking, the gluten is sufficiently developed and you are done kneading. If it tears, continue to knead the dough for a few more minutes, then check it again. Don't worry—it is hard to overknead bread dough by hand.*

recipe continues

MIXING AND KNEADING BY MACHINE: Combine the water, yeast, malt syrup, and starter in the mixer bowl. Whisk to mix completely before attaching the bowl to the machine. Fit the mixer with a dough hook attachment.

In a separate bowl, combine half of the bread flour, the salt, and the sugar. Add this to the water-starter mixture and mix on low speed until combined. Add most of the remaining bread flour and mix until the dough is quite firm but not dry. Increase the mixer speed to medium-low and knead for 5 to 8 minutes. The dough should be smooth and elastic, wrapping around the dough hook and leaving the sides of the bowl clean. (You can use the windowpane test, page 16, to check for gluten development.) When the dough is ready, remove the dough hook and remove the bowl from the machine. Cover the bowl with plastic wrap or a clean, damp kitchen towel and set it aside at room temperature to ferment and rise.

FERMENTING THE DOUGH: Let the dough rise until it is about 1½ times its original size, between 2 and 4 hours depending on the warmth of the room.

SHAPING THE BAGELS: When the dough has risen enough, turn it out on a clean, unfloured board or work surface. Dust a baking sheet with the semolina.

Cut the dough into eight 4-ounce pieces with a dough cutter or knife. Take one piece and use both hands to roll it into a rope about 10 inches long. Wrap the rope around one hand, allowing both ends to overlap on your palm. Roll your dough-covered palm on the surface to seal the ends together and make a uniformly round bagel with a 3-inch center hole. (If you have large hands, you may need to wrap the rope around only three of your fingers so that the center is not too big.) Place the shaped bagel on the baking sheet and repeat with the remaining pieces of dough.

Cover the baking sheet loosely with plastic wrap. Refrigerate for at least 8 hours or overnight. (This slow rise develops flavor.)

recipe continues

BOILING AND BAKING THE BAGELS: Preheat the oven to 450°F. Grease a clean baking sheet and set it aside next to the stove. Pull the bagels out of the refrigerator and check to see that they are larger and a bit more puffy than when they went in. If not, leave them out at room temperature, covered, until they start to inflate.

Fill a wide pot two-thirds full of water and bring it to a boil. Drop two bagels semolina-side up in the water. If all is right, they should float. After 15 seconds, use a spider or slotted spoon to turn them over. After another 15 seconds, pull them out of the water and transfer them to the greased baking sheet. (Boiling longer will give the bagel a tough outer crust.) Repeat the process with the rest of the bagels, leaving 2 inches between them on the pan.

As soon as the baking sheet is full, immediately place it on the middle rack of the oven and reduce the oven heat to 425°F. Bake for 12 to 15 minutes, rotating the baking sheet halfway through to ensure even baking. They are done when the tops have a golden sheen and bottoms are brown.

Let cool at room temperature. Store in a resealable plastic bag at room temperature for up to 3 days or freeze to store for up to a month. Defrost in the bag at room temperature. To reinvigorate the crust, place the bagels on a baking sheet and toast in a 350 °F oven for 5 to 7 minutes, or until warm and crusty.

If you haven't eaten your bagels after a few days, turn them into Bagel Chips (page 24), which last much longer than fresh bagels.

Everything Bagel Mix

When we started BernBaum's, we were boiling on a 1960s electric stove salvaged from the basement of family friend Heather Neis. There was only one baking oven, so we kept it classic and simple—just plain and seeded bagels. We expanded the restaurant, but we never saw the need to expand the bagel flavors in the end.

To use this Everything Bagel Mix, pour some onto a rimmed plate or pie plate. Place a just–boiled but not baked bagel top down in the mix to coat it. Return the bagel to the greased baking sheet coated side up and bake as directed on page 21. We found that seeded bagels take a few minutes longer to bake than the plain ones.

Makes 1 scant cup, enough for 12 bagels

½ cup natural or white sesame seeds

¼ cup nigella seeds* or poppy seeds

2 tablespoons flaky sea salt (such as Maldon)

1 tablespoon dried minced garlic

Nigella may be labeled as "kalonji" at your local international foods market.

Mix the sesame seeds, nigella seeds, salt, and garlic in a bowl. Store in a covered container for up to 2 weeks or freeze for up to a month.

Chagels

This is a chocolate bagel concocted by my brother–in–law Irad Eyal. I normally don't go for sweet bagels, but this one is good. What makes them better is that the chocolate is confined to an inner tunnel in the bread, à la chocolate croissants, so you don't end up with melted goo all over your fingers. These are best eaten plain, or maybe with a little good butter.

Makes 8 Chagels

1 batch Bagel dough (page 14), fermented and ready for shaping

1 cup high-quality bittersweet chocolate chips or chunks
   (preferably 50 to 60% cacao)

Flaky sea salt (such as Maldon)

Cut the bagel dough into eight 4-ounce portions. One at a time, roll a portion of dough into a rope. Press 2 tablespoons of the chocolate chips along the length of the rope. Roll the sides of the rope together to hide the chips in the middle. Close and roll into a bagel following the instructions for shaping on page 18. Repeat with the remaining portions of dough and chocolate. Cover the baking sheet and refrigerate the Chagels overnight.

The next morning, follow the boiling and baking instructions on page 21. Just before baking the Chagels, sprinkle each with a generous pinch of sea salt.

Store in a resealable plastic bag at room temperature for up to 3 days or freeze to store for up to a month. Defrost in the bag at room temperature. To reinvigorate the crust, place the bagels on a baking sheet and toast in a 350°F oven for 5 to 7 minutes, or until warm and crusty.

Bagel Chips

The sad thing about our bagels is that they don't have a long shelf life. However, a bagel chip does, and it uses up any day-old bagels. The chips are a great dipping tool for Hummus (see page 63) and Schmears (page 71), as well as being easy to eat alone.

The most tedious and difficult recipes were my father's purview, and this one is no exception. He mastered the bagel chip and kept us stocked with 30 to 40 pans per week. When my dad was baking at the restaurant, he would set out little plates of the just-baked snacks for those of us working.

Makes about 120 chips

> 8 leftover bagels (at least a day old)
> ¼ to ½ cup canola oil
> 2 tablespoons Everything Bagel Mix (page 22)
> 1 tablespoon kosher salt (any brand)

Preheat the oven to 325°F.

With the bagel flat on a work surface, slice vertically to make ¼-inch-thick pieces and place on two baking sheets in a single layer. Brush the tops liberally with canola oil and sprinkle evenly with Everything Bagel Mix and salt. Bake for 7 minutes, then rotate the pans and continue to bake until golden, about another 5 to 7 minutes.

Transfer the chips to a wire cooling rack and cool to room temperature. They will crisp up as they cool, so don't worry if they are slightly soft when you remove them from the oven.

Store in a resealable plastic bag or covered container for up to a month.

Focaccia

Another of our daily breads, this one is a pleasing and simple antidote to the bagel project. It takes about 10 minutes to put the dough together and another 10 to bake when you're ready. It is great for sandwiches, dipping, just eating plain, and makes the best Croutons (page 221).

Makes 4 or 5 buns, or 1 sheet about 13 × 9 inches

> 1 cup (8 ounces) water, body temperature*
>
> 1 teaspoon active dry yeast
>
> 2 cups (10 ounces) unbleached bread flour, plus more if needed
>
> 1 teaspoon Diamond Crystal kosher salt or ½ teaspoon other kosher salt
>
> 2 tablespoons extra virgin olive oil
>
> 1 tablespoon minced fresh herbs (optional)
>
> 1 tablespoon flaky sea salt (such as Maldon)
>
> *95 to 100°F; you can't feel a temperature change when you stick your finger in it.

Combine the water and yeast in a large bowl and whisk until the yeast is dissolved. Add 1 cup of the flour and whisk until pretty smooth, about 2 minutes. Add most of the remaining flour and the kosher salt. Stir with a spatula, wooden spoon, or your gloved hands to incorporate all the flour into a very wet dough. Depending on the specific conditions of your ingredients and kitchen, you may be okay with less flour *or* need to add the rest of the flour (or even a little more).

Cover the bowl with plastic wrap or a clean, damp kitchen towel and let the dough rise until doubled—1½ hours in a warm place, 3 hours in a cool one, or overnight in the refrigerator.

Preheat the oven to 450°F. Grease a baking sheet with the olive oil.

TO MAKE INDIVIDUAL FOCACCIA BUNS: Grease your hands and grab a piece of dough the size of a mandarin orange (about 2¼ inches diameter or 4 ounces) and plop it on the baking sheet. Repeat with the rest of the dough, spacing the pieces a

few inches apart. Once they are all on the pans, turn each piece over so that both sides are shiny from olive oil. Loosely form each piece into a ball, flatten slightly as you set it on the pan, and top each bun with herbs and a sprinkle of sea salt. Bake for 8 to 10 minutes on the middle rack of the oven, until golden. Rotate the baking sheets halfway through (after about 4 minutes) to ensure even baking.

TO MAKE A FOCACCIA SHEET: Pour the dough onto the greased baking sheet and turn it over to fully coat it with olive oil. With your fingertips, spread the dough to the corners of the pan. Use your fingers to dimple the surface (to create pockets for the toppings) and add an additional splash of olive oil. Top with the herbs and sea salt. Bake for 10 to 12 minutes on the middle rack of the oven, until browned on the edges and golden on the top. Rotate the baking sheet halfway through (after about 5 minutes) to ensure even baking.

Let cool on the baking sheet(s) and serve warm or at room temperature.

Store the cooled bread in a sealed container or resealable plastic bag. Focaccia lasts about 2 days on the counter, or up to a month in the freezer.

Challah

We once received a complaint that we had lied about our challah. The caller believed that we were trying to pass off brioche, instead of making the Jewish version. While I don't see how that would be a crime, this is not brioche since it has only about a third of the butter. We served our challah as a sandwich base or as a dinner roll. Start this early in the day so you can have it ready for dinner.

Makes 6 or 7 rolls, or 1 large braid for 12 good slices

¼ cup (2 ounces) milk, body temperature*

½ cup (4 ounces) water, body temperature

2 teaspoons active dry yeast**

3 cups + 2 tablespoons (1 pound) unbleached white bread flour, plus more for kneading

¼ cup (2 ounces) granulated sugar

1 tablespoon Diamond Crystal kosher salt or 1½ teaspoons other kosher salt

2 large eggs + 2 large egg yolks, beaten together

2 tablespoons butter, room temperature

Neutral oil or nonstick baking spray, for greasing

1 large egg beaten with 1 tablespoon water, for egg wash

1½ tablespoons sesame or poppy seeds (optional)

*95 to 100°F; you can't feel a temperature change when you stick your finger in it.

**This is just a little under the standard envelope.

recipe continues

Combine the milk and water and whisk in yeast. Let sit until foamy, 5 to 8 minutes.

Whisk together the flour, sugar, and salt in a large bowl or the bowl of a stand mixer until thoroughly combined.

MIXING AND KNEADING BY HAND: Add the yeast mixture, eggs and egg yolks, and butter to the flour mixture. Stir with a wooden spoon or spatula until it becomes too stiff to mix easily. Continue to mix with your floured hands until well combined. Turn the dough out onto a lightly floured board and knead for 10 to 15 minutes (or even longer) by hand. The dough should be smooth and elastic.

You can also judge if the dough is ready by temperature: It should be between 78° and 80°F when it has been sufficiently kneaded.

MIXING AND KNEADING BY MACHINE: Add the yeast mixture, eggs and egg yolks, and butter to the flour mixture in the mixer bowl. Fit the mixer with a dough hook attachment. Mix the dough on low speed for 2 to 3 minutes, until all ingredients are well-incorporated. Turn off the mixer and scrape down the sides of the bowl with a spatula. Turn the mixer back on and mix for another 5 to 6 minutes, until the dough is smooth and elastic and reaches 78° to 80°F.

When the dough is fully kneaded, grease a clean large bowl. Transfer the dough to the bowl and cover with plastic wrap or a clean, damp flour sack towel. Place in a warmish spot and let ferment (rise) for 1 to 2 hours, until it reaches 1½ times its original size.

Grease a baking sheet or line it with parchment paper.

FORMING ROLLS: Place the dough on a clean counter or butcher block. Using a dough cutter or knife, cut it into 6 or 7 even portions. To make the rolls round, cup one hand loosely over the dough and move your hand in a circle until it is tightens to a tidy sphere. Place the rolls on the prepared baking sheet about 3 inches apart.

FORMING A THREE-STRAND BRAID: This is exactly like braiding hair. Divide the dough into three equal portions on a clean counter. Roll each portion into a rope that is slightly wider in the center than the ends, cigar-shaped, about 16 inches long. Lay the ropes with one end touching and pinch that end together. Separate the outer ropes so they radiate out from the middle rope at an angle of about 30 degrees. Starting with the top rope, lift and fold it over the middle rope. Then lift and fold the bottom rope over the middle rope. Continue folding the top over the middle, then the bottom over the middle, until you reach the ends of the ropes. Pinch the loose ends together to keep them from unraveling and place the loaf on the baking sheet.

Cover loosely with plastic wrap. Let the rolls or braid rise at room temperature until they start to plump, about 30 minutes for rolls and up to an hour for a braid.

(If you won't be baking the challah right away, cover the rolls or braid on the baking sheet with plastic wrap and refrigerate for up to 8 hours. Make sure to let them plump for 30 minutes at room temperature before you bake them.)

While the challah is rising, preheat the oven to 350°F.

When you're ready to bake, brush the egg wash gently on the sides and top of the rolls or braid with a pastry brush or your hand. If you like, sprinkle poppy or sesame seeds on top.

Bake the rolls for 8 to 10 minutes, rotating the baking sheet after 5 minutes to bake evenly. Bake the braid for 18 to 20 minutes, rotating after 10 minutes. The challah is done when it is a deep golden brown and reaches an internal temperature of 185°F on an instant-read thermometer. Rest on a wire cooling rack for at least 45 minutes before slicing.

Challah keeps for up to 4 days in a sealed plastic bag or container at room temperature. It freezes beautifully, well wrapped, for up to a month.

Kalamata Olive Baguette

This is a fan favorite and holdover recipe from my previous restaurant, Green Market. It was adapted from one of my first and favorite baking books, Suzanne Dunaway's *No Need to Knead*. This recipe is forgiving and incredibly simple to make. A friend called it a salt lick for humans—it can be enjoyed as such, or as an accompaniment to cheese and meat platters, entree salads, or pasta.

Makes 2 baguettes

> 1¼ cups (10 ounces) water, body temperature*
>
> 2 teaspoons active dry yeast
>
> 5 cups (25 ounces) bread flour
>
> ¾ cup + 2 tablespoons (4 ounces) chopped and pitted
>   kalamata olives**
>
> ¾ cup (6 ounces) olive brine or a mix of brine and water
>
> 1 teaspoon Diamond Crystal kosher salt or ½ teaspoon other kosher salt
>
> 2 tablespoons extra virgin olive oil, for greasing and brushing
>
> 1 tablespoon flaky sea salt (such as Maldon)

**95 to 100°F; you can't feel a temperature change when you stick your finger in it.*

***I chop the olives in a mini food processor or with a knife. Once they are coarsely chopped, I set aside all but 2 tablespoons, and then process those 2 tablespoons to a paste.*

Whisk the water and yeast together in a large bowl until the yeast is dissolved. Add half of the bread flour and whisk for 3 to 4 minutes, until well blended. Add the chopped olives, olive paste, and olive brine, and whisk until combined. Add the kosher salt and the rest of the flour. Use a spatula, a wooden spoon, or your gloved hands to stir until uniformly mixed. Shape the dough into a ball in the bowl and cover with plastic wrap. Let sit at room temperature to ferment (rise), 1 to 2 hours, until the dough is 1½ times its original size.

When nicely proofed, cut the dough (in the bowl) into two equal portions. Grease a baguette pan (preferred) or large baking sheet. Oil your hands and plop one half of the dough into each of the baguette forms. (It is a very wet dough, so you will need to stretch and shape it in the baguette form.) If using a baking sheet, stretch out half

the dough, twist it to make a long cylinder, and place it on one side of the sheet. Repeat with the second half of the dough and place it 3 inches away from the first. Brush both baguettes with olive oil and generously sprinkle with sea salt. Loosely cover with plastic wrap and let the dough rise at room temperature until it starts to puff, 1 to 1½ hours.

Preheat the oven to 500°F. When the baguettes have puffed, unwrap the pan and place it on the middle rack of the oven. Bake for 5 minutes, then reduce the heat to 450°F. Continue to bake for another 15 to 20 minutes, rotating the pan after about 8 minutes for even baking, until the baguettes are lightly browned all over.

Place the bread, still on the pan, on a wire rack to cool. Let cool 1 hour before slicing.

Store in a resealable plastic bag or container for up to 3 days or freeze for up to a month.

Flax Crackers

We used to cater a lot at my previous restaurant, Green Market, and this was a recipe we added to complement our cheese boards. We originally rolled these out by hand. We have a video of my father, fully accessorized with a 1970s sweatband, laboring over flax cracker dough. We graduated to a small motorized pasta machine when we realized that no one besides my faithful dad would be willing to hand roll. We eventually made them with a very old and large dough sheeter that we bought at a bakery auction; I recommend a dough sheeter if you want to make 20 times this recipe. Otherwise, a pasta roller (either hand–cranked or a mixer attachment) or rolling pin works pretty well.

Makes roughly 160 crackers

> 2 cups + 6 tablespoons (12 ounces) all-purpose flour,
>   plus more for rolling
>
> 6 tablespoons (2 ounces) whole wheat flour
>
> ¾ cup (roughly 4 ounces) whole brown flaxseeds
>
> 1 tablespoon Diamond Crystal kosher salt
>   or 1½ teaspoons other kosher salt
>
> 1 teaspoon baking powder
>
> 2 teaspoons ground cumin
>
> 4 tablespoons (½ stick) unsalted butter,
>   cut into 1-inch squares, room temperature
>
> 1 cup (8 ounces) buttermilk, plus 1 tablespoon if needed,
>   especially if using a rolling pin
>
> ½ cup (4 ounces) extra virgin olive oil
>
> Up to 2 tablespoons flaky sea salt (such as Maldon)

Combine the all-purpose flour, whole wheat flour, flaxseeds, kosher salt, baking powder, and cumin in a large bowl or the bowl of a stand mixer. Whisk together well.

MIXING BY HAND: Cut in the butter with a pastry cutter or fork until the dough is the texture of coarse meal. Pour in the buttermilk and knead by hand to make a soft, uniform dough.

MIXING BY MACHINE: Fit the mixer with the paddle attachment. Add the butter while mixing on low speed. When the dough is the texture of coarse meal, pour in the buttermilk and continue to mix on low until a uniform ball of dough forms.

With either method, you may need to add 1 tablespoon of buttermilk if the dough isn't holding together. A softer dough is easier to roll out thinly.

Preheat the oven to 375°F. Line four 13 × 18-inch baking sheets with parchment paper. (If you only have one or two, don't worry; you'll be able to reuse them for the other batches.)

Lightly flour a work surface or board. Transfer the dough to the surface and cut it into quarters. Each of the quarters should weigh about 7 ounces. Cover three of the dough portions with a clean flour sack towel or plastic wrap.

With a rolling pin, roll one portion of the dough into a flattish rectangle about ½ inch thick, no wider than your pasta roller. Flour both sides. Starting on the widest setting, feed the dough through the pasta roller. Change the roller setting to the next thinner size and put the dough through again. Continue doing this until the dough is about 1/16 inch thick. (If you are using a rolling pin instead of pasta roller, roll the dough to 1/16 inch thick.) Place the dough on a prepared baking sheet. If the dough is longer than your sheet, cut to fit and place each length side by side on the baking sheet. (Do not overlap.) Repeat with the remaining dough portions for as many baking sheets as you have.

Generously brush the dough with the olive oil, either with your gloved hand or a brush. Sprinkle evenly with the sea salt. Use a pizza cutter or knife to cut the dough into 2-inch squares (or whatever size and shape you would like).

Place one baking sheet on a lower rack and another on an upper rack of the oven and bake 7 minutes. Rotate the pans and bake another 7 to 10 minutes or until golden and fragrant. Depending on how even your oven heat is, you may have to move the center crackers to the edges during baking to ensure that all of the crackers are evenly cooked. Transfer the crackers, still on the parchment paper, to a wire rack to cool; break them apart once cool. If you need to reuse a baking sheet, let it cool it down, then line it with clean parchment paper and add the next batch of cracker dough.

Store in a sealed container for 3 weeks or more.

Pat McCoy looking dapper at her "Soul Food + Bubbly" dinner
at BernBaum's, New Year's Eve 2022.

Sourdough Rye for Beginners

When BernBaum's was just a few people with barely a kitchen, we made this bread for the brisket sandwich.

Remember to feed your starter 1 to 2 hours before you start the recipe. Measure out what you need and store the rest. This recipe extends over 2 days.

You have two options for baking: a covered Dutch oven (recommended) or a baking sheet.

Makes one 9-inch loaf, for 12 good slices

> 1¼ cups (10 ounces) active Sourdough Starter (page 11)*
>
> 1½ cups (12 ounces) water, body temperature**
>
> ½ teaspoon active dry yeast
>
> 1⅞ to 2 cups (10 ounces) unbleached bread flour
>
> Scant 1½ cups (6 ounces) medium rye flour
>
> 1½ teaspoons Diamond Crystal kosher salt
>   or ¾ teaspoon other kosher salt
>
> 1 teaspoon caraway seeds, toasted
>
> Neutral oil or nonstick baking spray, for greasing
>
> Boiling water
>
> *One way to check that your starter is active and ready is to drop a teaspoonful into a cup of cold water. If it floats, it is ready.*
> **95° to 100°F; you can't feel a temperature change when you stick your finger in it.*

Combine the starter, water, and yeast in a large bowl. Let sit for 5 minutes, then whisk to ensure that it is well mixed. Add the bread flour and rye flour and use your gloved hands to mix until a wet dough comes together; this should take about 5 minutes. Cover the bowl with plastic wrap or a clean, damp flour sack towel and let sit for 20 minutes to let the dough rest. This allows the gluten to start developing and is crucial for texture.

recipe continues

Sprinkle the salt and caraway seeds over the dough. Knead the dough for 3 to 5 minutes, until the salt and caraway are fully incorporated. Grease a clean large bowl and place the dough in it. Cover with plastic wrap. Let the dough ferment (rise) for an hour, until about 1½ times its original size.

Wet your hands with water so that they don't stick to the dough. Uncover the bowl and pull the right side of the dough (at 3 o'clock) gently towards the left side of the dough, folding it over ❶. Next pull the top of the dough (at 12 o'clock) towards the bottom ❷. Pull the left side (9 o'clock) towards the right, and finally pull the closest edge of the dough (6 o'clock) towards the top ❸. These gentle folds trap gases in the dough and gently help in creating a light and well-structured final product. Recover the bowl and let sit 45 minutes to an hour, until it has increased to 1½ times its current size.

Repeat the folding 3 more times. After the last fold, cover it with plastic wrap, and refrigerate overnight.

If you only fold and turn the dough twice, you will still get a nice bread—just a little heavier.

The next morning, pull the bowl out of the refrigerator and let the dough warm up for about 30 minutes. Flour a sheet of parchment paper ❹.

Take the dough out of the bowl and place it on the clean counter or board. Gently stretch it into a rectangle about 9 × 11inches. Carefully fold the left and right ends in and then roll the dough, starting at the bottom, into a log. Use your fingers to seal the seam.

Place the loaf seam side down on the parchment paper ❺.

Cover loosely with plastic wrap and let rise until it is 1½ times its original size (1 to 1½ hours, depending on the warmth of the kitchen).

Preheat the oven to 450°F. If you'll be using a baking sheet, place a cast-iron skillet or other heavy pan on the bottom rack of the oven. Right before baking, flour and score the top of the loaf with a sharp knife ❻.

recipe continues

BAKING IN A DUTCH OVEN: Preheat the Dutch oven, without the cover, on the middle rack of the oven for at least 15 minutes. Once it is heated, remove the pot (taking care not to burn yourself!), place the loaf (still on the parchment) inside, cover it, and return the pot to the oven. Bake for 15 minutes. Uncover the pot and bake for 25 to 40 minutes more, until the loaf is dark brown with a nice crust. (It will be 190°F in its center when checked with an instant-read thermometer.)

BAKING ON A BAKING SHEET: Place the loaf, still on the parchment atop the baking sheet, and set the baking sheet on the middle rack. Pour 1 cup boiling water into the cast-iron pan on the bottom rack. Bake for 15 minutes. Turn the oven down to 400°F, rotate the baking sheet, and bake an additional 25 to 40 minutes, until the loaf is dark brown with a nice crust. (It will be 190°F in its center when checked with an instant-read thermometer.)

Remove from the oven and place the pan or Dutch oven on a wire cooling rack. Cool for at least an hour before slicing.

Store in a resealable plastic bag for up to 4 days, or freeze for up to a month.

Aunt Joyce's Buns

My dad's oldest sister, Joyce, was a formidable baker and party girl—an uncommon combination of attributes, but charming nonetheless. When I was a teenage jerk, she lived with us for a while. She was the only grownup willing to sit on folding chaises in the driveway and sunbathe with me while I burned myself to a crisp. She enjoyed country music, dancing, and skimpy clothes well into her dotage. And, although she didn't eat much, she could cook. (She always managed to skip out on the cleanup, though.) These are a great Midwestern roll for dinner or sandwiches. They could be made heartier by substituting some of the all-purpose flour with whole grain flour, but some things aren't meant to be healthy.

Makes about 8 buns

> 1½ teaspoons active dry yeast
>
> ¼ teaspoon + scant ½ cup (3¼ ounces) granulated sugar
>
> 1 cup water, body temperature*
>
> 1 teaspoon Diamond Crystal kosher salt or ½ teaspoon other kosher salt
>
> 2½ tablespoons vegetable oil, plus more for greasing
>
> 1 large egg, beaten
>
> 2½ cups (12.5 ounces) all-purpose flour, plus more if needed
>
> 2 tablespoons butter, melted, for brushing tops of buns (optional)
>
> *95° to 100°F; you can't feel a temperature change when you stick your finger in it.*

Whisk the yeast, ¼ teaspoon of the sugar, and 1½ tablespoons of the water together in a small bowl. Let stand 10 minutes, until foamy.

Meanwhile, mix the remaining sugar, salt, oil, the remaining water, and the egg together in a large bowl. Add the yeast mixture and stir well. Stir in 2 cups of the flour until well mixed. Stir in the remaining ½ cup flour, then knead the dough with your gloved hands until it makes a sticky dough. Add more flour as needed to make a soft, evenly mixed dough. (You don't want to add too much flour, as it will take away from the light texture.) Cover the dough with plastic wrap and let rise for 1 to 1½ hours, until doubled in size.

Aunt Joyce. Even her hairdo is frothy.

Grease a baking sheet. Plop the dough onto the clean counter with a dough scraper or spatula. Portion the dough into about 8 equal-size buns (about 3 ounces each). Roll each portion into a smooth ball: Place your hand loosely over the ball and roll it against your cupped fingers and the counter to round it. Place the balls on the baking sheet about 3 inches apart. Cover with a clean flour sack towel or loose plastic wrap. Let rise for another 45 minutes to an hour, until 1½ times original size.

While the buns are rising, preheat the oven to 375°F.

Place the baking sheet of buns on the middle rack of the oven and bake for 14 to 16 minutes. Rotate the baking sheet after about 7 minutes for even baking. They should be golden brown on the top and pillowy when they are perfectly baked.

Remove from the oven and brush with melted butter, if you would like a shiny top. Serve immediately or transfer the buns to a wire rack to cool.

Store in a resealable plastic bag for up to 4 days, or freeze for up to a month.

Knishes

Although "knish" pronunciation might strain the Midwestern tongue—the *k* isn't silent—their crowd-pleasing flavor is easily understood. There are as many recipes for knishes as there are mispronunciations. We chose to go the French way (like Brett's mom) and use puff pastry with lots of butter in it, rather than an oil-based kosher dough, and baked, not fried. As for shape, we made little round puffs, open on the top. But you are welcome to experiment and make them round or square, open or closed, which are other popular options.

One beautiful thing about knishes is that they freeze well and a big batch can provide dinner or lunch for more than one day—which is good, because they're a bit of a project, especially with homemade puff dough. Feel free to substitute ingredients in the filling recipes—as long as it sticks together enough to be spooned onto the dough, it will work.

Puff Dough

The recipe that inspired my fealty to puff dough (after culinary school didn't) was from Michel Richard's *Happy in the Kitchen*. Over the years, I have adapted his recipe for many uses and love its scalability and relative ease. I don't see the efficacy of making less than this amount of dough—same work for less product. It will give you enough for a couple batches of knishes, or other items such as a decadent take on pizza, palmier cookies, or tart shells.

Makes enough puff dough for 28 to 30 knishes

3¾ cups (18½ ounces) all-purpose flour
  + up to ½ cup for dusting the counter

1 tablespoon Diamond Crystal kosher salt
  or 1½ teaspoons other kosher salt

Up to 1½ cups (12 ounces) ice water

1 pound (4 sticks) unsalted butter,
  each stick cut in half lengthwise*

**The butter should not be too chilled,
  but also not too soft; it needs to be workable
  with a rolling pin, like Play-Doh.*

The hardest thing about puff dough is keeping everything at the right temperature for folding, which gives puff dough its layers and amazing texture. So if it is 90°F in your kitchen, I recommend buying puff dough—it's too frustrating to spend the effort and time without the results. Otherwise, go for it!

recipe continues

Whisk 3¾ cups flour and the salt together in a large bowl. Slowly add ice water while mixing with your hand to form a sticky, craggy dough. Use as little water as you can. Knead for a few minutes until the lumps smooth out and it's uniformly mixed. (This is known as the détrempe.) Wrap in plastic and let rest for 1 hour or up to 1 day in the refrigerator ❶.

Cut two large sheets of parchment paper. Lay the butter slices on one sheet in a rectangle four pieces across by two wide. Cover with the other sheet of parchment and lightly roll the butter with a rolling pin to form a uniform rectangle roughly 6 × 10 inches and ½ inch thick, with even edges; if they get flattened and uneven, just smush the butter back into a rectangle with your fingers.

Dust the counter with some of the extra flour. Plop the détrempe on the counter and lightly flour the top. Roll it into an 18 × 18-inch square.

Remove the top sheet of parchment from the butter slab. Turn it over and place on the détrempe at a 45-degree angle, centered on the square. Remove the parchment from the top of butter ❷.

Brush off excess flour from the dough with a pastry brush. Fold in each corner of the détrempe to cover the butter. Brush off any flour from the top of the détrempe after each fold ❸.

Roll out the dough-butter package to a rectangle roughly 14 × 20 inches ❹.

FIRST TURN: Turn the dough package with the long edge parallel to the edge of the counter. Brush off any flour from top of dough. Fold the right one-third of the dough over the middle third ❺.

Brush off excess flour again. Bring the left third of the dough over the middle third, to the edge (like folding a letter) ❻. You should have a compact rectangle about 14 × 7 inches. Cover the dough with a clean, dry kitchen towel. Rest the dough for 20 minutes to let the gluten relax. (If your kitchen is very warm, place the dough package on a parchment paper–covered baking sheet, cover, and refrigerate it for about 15 minutes, then leave it out on the counter for at least 5 minutes before the next turn.)

recipe continues

SECOND THROUGH SIXTH TURNS: Turn the dough so that the seam edge (from the left side that you folded over) is parallel to the edge of the counter. Roll out the dough to a 10 × 20-inch rectangle. Again fold the right third over the middle, brush off excess flour, then fold over the left third. Cover and rest the dough for at least 30 minutes. Repeat five times.

> *Sometimes you can get two turns in before resting.*
> *If after the first turn, it's easy to roll the dough out to 10 × 20 again,*
> *feel free to get in another turn in before resting.*

When the six turns are complete, place the dough with the long edge parallel to the counter and cut the dough into 3 equal portions, roughly 3 × 6 inches. Double-wrap each portion in plastic wrap. Refrigerate for at least 2 hours, up to 2 days, or freeze for up to a month. If you freeze it, defrost it in the fridge for 6 hours or up to 2 days before using.

Potato and Caramelized Onion Knish Filling

The classic knish is just mashed potato in pastry and not exactly a flavor bomb. The simple additions of lemon, dill, and caramelized onion work wonders on this dish.

Makes about 1½ cups, enough to fill 6 to 8 knishes

CARAMELIZED ONIONS

3 medium yellow onions (about 18 ounces total),
  root and stem ends trimmed, peeled, and halved from root to stem

2 tablespoons unsalted butter or canola oil

1 teaspoon Diamond Crystal kosher salt
  or ½ teaspoon other kosher salt

1 sprig fresh thyme or rosemary, or ⅛ teaspoon dried (optional)

Place each onion half flat on the cutting board and cut from root to stem into ¼-inch-wide strips. You should have about 2½ cups of onions. (If you wind up with more, just add them too.)

Heat a wide-bottomed pot over medium-high heat. Add the butter or oil. If using butter, wait until it foams. Add the onions and stir to coat them with fat. Sprinkle with the salt, add the herbs (if using), and reduce heat to medium or low. Cook the onions at a gentle pace and with regular stirring for at least 20 minutes. They will first turn translucent before starting to brown. Once they start to brown, they will want to stick and burn to the pan, so cover the pan for about 30 seconds to trap the steam. Uncover, stir well, and continue cooking and stirring. Once the onions are a deep caramel (not black) and about one-quarter of their original volume, they are done; this should take 20 to 30 minutes longer. Remove from the heat and cool to room temperature.

This makes about ¾ cup caramelized onions. You can use them as a condiment (a nice ace up your sleeve for adding to a sandwich, burger, or cheese plate) as well as your next batches of knishes. Store them in a covered container in the refrigerator for up to 5 days, or freeze for up to a month; defrost in the refrigerator.

POTATO FILLING

3 or 4 medium red potatoes (12 ounces), scrubbed, and half-heartedly peeled (you want *some* peel)

1¾ teaspoons Diamond Crystal kosher salt or 1 teaspoon other kosher salt

2 tablespoons Caramelized Onions (above)

1½ teaspoons minced fresh dill

3 tablespoons heavy cream

1 tablespoon butter (preferably unsalted)*

½ teaspoon fresh lemon juice

2 or 3 turns of a pepper mill

If using salted butter, omit the salt.

Place the potatoes in a pot, cover with cold water by 1 inch, and add 1 teaspoon of the Diamond Crystal or ½ teaspoon other kosher salt. Bring to a simmer, cover, then reduce the heat to maintain a simmer until the potatoes are fully cooked and soft, about 15 minutes. (Stick a fork into a potato to see if it is cooked enough—you will need to mash them.) Drain in a colander, then pour onto a baking sheet and set aside to cool to room temperature.

Place the potatoes in a large bowl. Add the caramelized onions, dill, cream, butter, lemon juice, the remaining salt, and the pepper. Mash with a potato masher, sturdy whisk, or your gloved hands until everything is evenly mixed. (You can use a stand

recipe continues

mixer with a paddle attachment; just be careful not to overmix, which whips air into the potatoes and makes the filling gluey.) Taste and add more lemon juice, salt, and/or pepper if necessary.

If not using immediately, store in a covered container in the refrigerator for up to 5 days; do not freeze.

Shredded Root Vegetable Filling

This is the knish equivalent of a hearty vegetable borscht.

Makes about 1½ cups, enough to fill 6 to 8 knishes

> 1 medium carrot, peeled and ends trimmed
>
> 1 medium parsnip, peeled and ends trimmed
>
> One 4-inch-diameter beet, turnip, or rutabaga, peeled and ends trimmed*
>
> 5 tablespoons butter (preferably unsalted)**
>
> 1 small onion, peeled, root and stem ends trimmed, halved and sliced thin
>
> 1 clove garlic, peeled and minced
>
> 1 teaspoon minced fresh tender herbs (such as parsley, chives, tarragon, or dill), or ¼ teaspoon dried herbs (herbes de Provence, marjoram, and thyme are good options)
>
> 3 tablespoons all-purpose flour
>
> ¼ cup heavy cream, scalded***
>
> ¾ teaspoon Diamond Crystal kosher salt or ¼ teaspoon other kosher salt
>
> 1 or 2 turns of a pepper mill
>
> Splash of sherry vinegar

**You can certainly substitute for any root vegetables with others to your liking.*

***If using salted butter, reduce the salt by half.*

****The easiest way to scald the cream is by microwaving it for 30 to 60 seconds on high, until a skin forms on top.*

USING A FOOD PROCESSOR: Cut all the vegetables so they fit through the feed chute. Shred using the shredding disk.

USING A BOX GRATER: Shred all of the vegetables through the large holes of the grater into a large bowl.

Heat a wide-bottomed pot over medium-high heat. Add 1 tablespoon of the butter and let it melt. Once foamy, add the onion, garlic, and herbs. Sweat (cook without coloring) for 3 to 5 minutes, until the onions are translucent.

Add the shredded vegetables and continue to cook, stirring often, for another 5 minutes until the vegetables start to wilt. Move all of the vegetables to the perimeter of the pot. Add the remaining 4 tablespoons butter to the space in the center. Once it has melted, whisk in the flour to make a roux and cook for about a minute, until all of flour is absorbed in the butter. Continue to whisk while slowly pouring in the cream, then cook until it becomes a smooth, very thick sauce.

Stir the vegetables in from the sides and incorporate them into the sauce. Reduce the heat to medium-low and cook gently until the vegetables are just cooked but haven't become a mushy blob. Remove from heat and season with salt, pepper and vinegar. Pour into a shallow pan (like a casserole dish or pie plate) and let cool to room temperature. Once cool, the filling should be thick and hold its shape when scooped. If not using immediately, store in a covered container in the refrigerator for up to 5 days. Do not freeze.

Choose-Your-Own-Vegetarian-Adventure Filling

At the restaurant, we tended to create fillings based on the bits and bobs of vegetables and other vegetarian items that needed to be used up. I can assure you that almost anything can be made into a knish filling—we did potato, lentil, onion, and Gruyère cheese knishes and also chickpea, kale, and smoked carrot knishes. Knishes welcome leftovers and reward creativity.

Makes 1½ to 2 cups filling, enough to fill 6 to 8 knishes

> 6 tablespoons (¾ stick) butter,* or 4 tablespoons (½ stick) butter and 2 tablespoons neutral oil
>
> ½ cup chopped or thinly sliced peeled allium (such as onion, leek, scallion, and/or shallot)
>
> 1 clove garlic, peeled and minced
>
> 1 teaspoon minced fresh tender herbs or ¼ teaspoon dried herbs (your choice)
>
> 2 to 3 cups shredded or finely chopped raw vegetables, peeled first if necessary**
>
> 5 tablespoons all-purpose flour
>
> ½ cup heavy cream, scalded***
>
> 1 teaspoon Diamond Crystal kosher salt or ½ teaspoon other kosher salt
>
> 1 or 2 turns of a pepper mill
>
> ½ cup cheese bits (optional)

**If using salted butter, reduce or omit the salt.*

***Pay attention to the water content of the vegetables—tomatoes, mushrooms, or zucchini, for example, will give off more water than, say, carrots, and require longer cooking to evaporate the excess liquid.*

****The easiest way to scald the cream is by microwaving it for 30 to 60 seconds on high, until a skin forms on top.*

Heat a wide-bottomed pot over medium-high heat. Melt 2 tablespoons of the butter until it foams, or heat the oil. Add the allium, garlic, and herbs. Sweat (cook without coloring) for 3 to 5 minutes, until translucent.

Add the vegetables and continue to cook, stirring often, for another 5 minutes until the vegetables are cooked but not mushy. (If the vegetables have given off a lot of liquid, raise the heat briefly to evaporate. Return the heat to medium.)

THICKENING WITH A ROUX: Move all of the vegetables to the perimeter of the pot. Add the remaining 4 tablespoons butter to the space in the center. Once it has melted, whisk in the flour to make a roux and cook for about a minute, until the flour is completely absorbed. Continue to whisk while slowly pouring in the cream, and cook until it becomes a smooth, very thick sauce. Stir the vegetables in from the sides and incorporate them into the sauce. Add bits of cheese if you are using them, remove from the heat and season with salt and pepper. (If you are not using a roux, this is when you stir the mashed beans or cream cheese into the vegetables, mixing well.)

If you don't want to use the roux (the butter and flour mixture) and cream, mashed beans or cream cheese (really anything that can be turned into a paste) can hold the filling together instead.

Pour into a shallow pan (like a casserole dish or pie plate) and let cool to room temperature. Once cooled, the filling should be thick and hold its shape when scooped.

If not using immediately, store in a covered container in the refrigerator for up to 5 days. Do not freeze.

Salami Filling

We ordered wonderful charcuterie from Underground Meats in Madison, Wisconsin, which inspired this knish filling. It tastes like a very fancy hot dog.

Makes about 1½ cups filling, enough for 6 to 8 knishes

- 3 medium red-skinned potatoes (8 ounces), scrubbed and half-heartedly peeled (you want some peel in your mashed potatoes)
- 1½ teaspoons Diamond Crystal kosher salt
  or 1¼ teaspoons other kosher salt
- 1 tablespoon olive oil
- 1 small onion, peeled, ends trimmed, and finely chopped
- 1 clove garlic, peeled and minced
- 1 teaspoon herbes de Provence or Italian seasoning
- 2 ounces high-quality salami, diced small (½ cup)
- 8 cornichons or 4 small dill gherkins, finely chopped (2 tablespoons)
- 1 teaspoon mustard (preferably Dijon, but any mustard will do)
- 2 tablespoons heavy cream
- 2 teaspoons unsalted butter*
- 3 turns of a pepper mill

If using salted butter, omit the salt from the filling.

Place the potatoes in a pot, cover with cold water by 1 inch, and add 1 teaspoon of the salt. Bring to a simmer over medium-high heat, cover, and reduce the heat to maintain a simmer until the potatoes are fully cooked and soft, about 15 minutes. (Stick a fork into a potato to see if it is tender and cooked—you will need to mash them.) Drain in a colander, then pour onto a baking sheet and set aside to cool to room temperature.

Heat a sauté pan over medium-high heat. Add the olive oil. Once it is warm (it will look shimmery in the pan), add the onion, garlic, and herb seasoning. Cook for 3 to 5 minutes, reducing the heat if necessary, until the onion is translucent but not colored at all. Add the salami and continue to cook for a few more minutes, until hot but not crispy. Remove from the heat and let cool.

Place the potatoes and the onion mixture in a large bowl. Add the cornichons, mustard, cream, butter, the remaining salt, and the pepper. Mash with a potato masher, a sturdy whisk, or your gloved hands until everything is evenly mixed. (You can also use a stand mixer with a paddle attachment; just be careful not to overmix, which makes a gluey filling and an uglier knish.) Taste and season again with salt and pepper if needed.

If not using immediately, store in a covered container in the refrigerator for up to 5 days. Do not freeze.

Finishing the Knishes

If you are the kind of person who loves to fold napkins or make origami, then finishing knishes is for you!

Makes 6–8 knishes

> 1 large egg
> 1 tablespoon water
> Flour, for dusting
> ¼ batch Puff Dough (page 44)
> 1 batch filling of your choice
> Nonstick baking spray (optional)

recipe continues

Preheat the oven to 400°F, or 375°F if using convection. Line a baking sheet with parchment paper or spray it with nonstick baking spray. Whisk together the egg and water to make an egg wash. Set it aside.

Lightly flour a clean counter or board. Place the puff dough atop the flour, long side parallel to the edge facing you. Roll the strip until it is ½ inch thick and about 24 inches long, then turn it 90 degrees and roll until it is about 6 inches wide. The dough should now be a little under ¼ inch thick ❶. (Don't roll it too thin as you will smush the flakiness potential of the puff dough.)

Place the rolled-out dough strip with the long side parallel to the counter edge. Brush egg wash along the top quarter of the strip. With a 2-ounce scoop or ¼-cup measure, scoop a level amount of filling and place it in the center of the dough strip, just under the egg wash, 1½ inches from one end of the strip. Continue to scoop and place filling along the center line of the strip, leaving 1½ inches between dollops, until you are within 1½ inches of the far end ❷.

Fold the bottom edge of the dough up and over the filling, 1 inch below the egg-washed edge. Press the edge of the dough to seal it over the filling. Gently roll the filled dough over the egg-washed top margin, so the seam is underneath ❸.

Press down on the empty part of the dough down with your index finger to seal it between each scoop of filling ❹. Use a bench scraper or knife to cut through the dough where you pressed it, cutting close to the right edge of the scoop of filling ❺. (This should allow for a 1-inch gap of sealed dough before the next scoop of filling.) Cut again right after the scoop of filling and repeat to the end of the strip. You should have 6 to 8 little pockets of dough, closed on the left side and open on the right side.

Fold each pocket to the left, so that open side is face up; pinch the sides all around to make a round shape like an open beggar's purse with the filling inside. You will be able to see a little filling within the crimped opening. Place the knishes 2 inches apart on the prepared baking sheet ❻.

Brush all sides of the knishes with the egg wash. Bake for 10 minutes on the middle rack of the oven. Rotate the pan for even baking, and bake for an additional 10 minutes or until the knishes are golden brown all over and the pastry is flaky. Serve immediately.

recipe continues

If not serving right away, cool the knishes completely on the baking sheet. Transfer to a covered container or resealable plastic bag and refrigerate for up to 4 days. You can also freeze them in a covered container or heavy-duty plastic bag for up to a month, and defrost in the refrigerator. To rewarm before serving, set them on a parchment paper–lined baking sheet and place in an oven at 350°F until hot and flaky, about 10 minutes.

Spreads, Pickles, and Relishes

After the labor of homemade bagels, breads, and crackers, it's a relief to get to the fun part—all the toppings. This chapter contains all I need to feed myself: a dip or a spread, good bread or crackers, and a crunchy–salty–pickled bite. Everyone loves a little nosh. Who needs to bother with a *meal* all the time? Plus, Jewish delis and the Nordic–German tables of the Midwest share the same devotion to pickle plates, so fermented foods were destined to play a starring role at BernBaum's.

Hummus

Hummus has come a long way since I discovered it in my college years in *The Silver Palate Cookbook*. I thought it was pronounced "humus" (like the soil layer), and my first version tasted like bland bean toothpaste. I know it's available at every gas station at this point, but making it from scratch does yield a more authentic sesame–tinged, citrus–bright flavor. I use dried beans as that is cheaper and tastier, but you can always use canned chickpeas, aka garbanzo beans, for a faster result—just skip to the blending step and be careful with the salt level. If you want an extra lemon kick, try drizzling it with Ladolemono (page 225), a simple vinaigrette of fresh lemon juice and extra virgin olive oil.

We served Hummus with everything from Bagels to our Flax Crackers and Bagel Chips. To serve, we topped it with a dusting of za'atar and extra virgin olive oil.

Makes about 1½ cups

⅔ cup (4 ounces) dried chickpeas

¼ teaspoon baking soda

1 clove garlic, unpeeled, smashed with the side of a knife blade

½ teaspoon kosher salt (any brand)

2 tablespoons + 2 teaspoons tahini (aka tehina—ground sesame paste)

2 cloves garlic, peeled and minced (1 teaspoon)

1 teaspoon Diamond Crystal kosher salt or ½ teaspoon other kosher salt

1 to 2 tablespoons fresh lemon juice

Tahini (aka tehina)—ground sesame paste—is usually available in the international section of most grocery stores, or any international food market that has Middle Eastern items. The same goes for za'atar, although I fully recommend Penzeys Spices (penzeys.com) for their version. If you want to go ultra premium, La Boîte (laboiteny.com) has a lovely version.

recipe continues

SOAKING: Soak the chickpeas in 2 cups water (roughly three times as much water as chickpeas) in a container large enough to roomily contain both, as the chickpeas double in size. Optimally, let them soak overnight or at least 12 hours.

COOKING: Drain the soaked chickpeas; you should have about 1¼ cups. Bring the chickpeas, 2 cups fresh water, the baking soda, and smashed garlic to a simmer in a medium pot. Add the ½ teaspoon salt and continue to simmer until fully cooked and soft, 30 to 40 minutes. You should have roughly 1¾ cups cooked chickpeas. Drain them in a colander. Fish out any garlic skin, as it won't blend.

BLENDING: Add the chickpeas, tahini, minced garlic, and salt to a food processor bowl or blender jar. Pulse to mix, then let the machine run for a few minutes. When the hummus is smooth like butter, add lemon juice to taste. (My palate runs to the very bright, so I add even more lemon.) If the hummus is too pasty or thick to process easily, add a few tablespoons water.

Store in a covered container in the refrigerator for up to a week.

Beet Hummus

After my first attempt at a menu for BernBaum's, Brett challenged me to make it more creative. Not for the first time in my life, I added beets. We used it on our vegetarian bagel plate with Baba Ghanoush, Apple–Cucumber Tabbouleh, and greens.

Although you can make hummus by adding a bunch of different vegetables, herbs, and/or nuts (even the unholy mashup of "chocolate dessert hummus" one can buy at Target), red beets provide great color on a plate and are a good marriage of Israeli and Midwestern ingredients. (I once tried carrot hummus, which unfortunately looks like vomit.) Beet hummus is a great dip for bagel chips and fresh vegetables. I add some to the side of a salad for an energy–fueled lunch.

While you can boil the beets, I like the slightly caramelized taste of a roasted beet.

Makes 3 cups

> 1 or 2 very large (4-inch diameter) red beets, or 2 to 4 smaller beets, root and stems trimmed, scrubbed
>
> 1 tablespoon oil (whatever is handy: canola, vegetable, olive oil)
>
> Kosher salt (any brand)
>
> 2 tablespoons + 2 teaspoons tahini (aka tehina—ground sesame paste)
>
> 2 cups drained cooked chickpeas
>
> 2 cloves garlic, peeled and minced
>
> 2 teaspoons ground sumac*
>
> 2 to 3 tablespoons fresh lemon juice (1 lemon)
>
> *Sumac is a Middle Eastern spice made of ground sumac berries. It adds tart flavor and a beautiful deep red to a dish. We found ours online or at a local international food market.*

Preheat the oven to 400°F. Line a baking pan with parchment paper or foil (for easy cleanup).

Cut the beets in half from the root to stem end. Toss them with the oil and a liberal sprinkle of salt. Place in the prepared baking pan cut side down. Roast until you can easily pierce them with a paring knife, 20 to 30 minutes depending upon the size of the beets. If you're using a mix of sizes, check the beets after 15 minutes; pull

recipe continues

out the smaller beets when done, and continue to roast the larger halves until they are fully cooked. (It is important to fully cook the beets so they will puree smoothly.) Remove from the oven and set aside to cool.

Peel the beet halves and cut them into chunks. You want 1 to 1½ cups of beet.

> *To peel beets, I use a paring knife to lop off the stub of the stem, then grab the beet skin between my knife and thumb and pull the skin off in sheets. You can peel small beets by just rubbing the skin with your gloved hands.*

Add the beets and tahini to a food processor bowl or blender jar. Process until pureed. Add the chickpeas, garlic, 2 to 3 teaspoons Diamond Crystal kosher salt or 1 to 1½ teaspoons other kosher salt, and the sumac and process for a few minutes, until the hummus is as smooth as you want it. While the machine is running, pour in lemon juice to taste and process until mixed. If the hummus is too thick, add a tablespoon or more of water and continue to blend.

Store in a covered container in the refrigerator for up to a week.

Baba Ghanoush

Baba ghanoush, the Levantine name for an eggplant spread, is another vegan flavor bomb and this one adds smoke and bright flavors to the maligned eggplant. The most important step is to char the eggplants, either over a gas burner (making a sticky mess of your stovetop) or a grill. You can also broil them in the oven. This is a perfect pairing with Hummus (page 63 or 65), Labne (page 76), and Zhug (page 105) on a mezze platter with vegetables or Bagel Chips (page 24). It works beautifully on a sandwich and with salad. I also serve it with lamb chops or other simple meat dishes.

Makes 1½ to 2 cups

> 1 globe eggplant (about 1 pound), washed
>
> Olive oil (optional)
>
> ½ teaspoon Diamond Crystal kosher salt,
>   or ¼ teaspoon other kosher salt
>
> 1 clove garlic, peeled and minced
>
> 2 tablespoons tahini (aka tehina—ground sesame paste)
>
> 2 to 3 tablespoons fresh lemon juice (1 lemon)

CHARRING UNDER THE BROILER: Halve the eggplant lengthwise. Brush the cut sides with olive oil, and sprinkle with salt. Place the halves cut side down on a baking sheet. Place a few inches under the broiler to char. Once the skin side is blackened, 5 minutes, turn the eggplant halves over and char the cut side for an additional 5 minutes. Remove the pan and turn the oven to 350°F.

recipe continues

CHARRING OVER A FLAME: If using a gas grill, heat it to 450°F. You can also do this over a gas stove burner. Place the eggplant across the grate over the flame, rotating it to blacken each side. This should take about 15 minutes. While the eggplant is charring, preheat the oven to 350°F. When all sides are charred, place the eggplant on a baking sheet.

Bake the eggplant until it is completely soft, about 5 to 8 minutes. (It doesn't hurt to overcook it.) Remove from the oven and set aside to cool.

Lightly chop the eggplant, including some of the skin but not the stem. Transfer to a large bowl or the bowl of a food processor. Add ½ teaspoon Diamond Crystal kosher salt or ¼ teaspoon other kosher salt, the garlic, tahini, and lemon juice. Mix in the bowl with a potato masher and spatula, or pulse in the food processor to make a semi-smooth paste. Taste and adjust the seasoning; you may want more lemon or salt, as I usually do.

Store in a covered container in the refrigerator for up to a week.

Whipped Tofu

For the vegans, we offered this simple spread to replace cream cheese on sandwiches and bagels.

This spread is very mild, and therefore needs a good flavor foil alongside it, like Smoked Carrot Lox (page 100) and Black Garlic Tehina (page 106).

Makes 1¼ cups

> One 14-ounce package firm tofu, drained
>
> 1 tablespoon rice vinegar
>
> ¾ teaspoon Diamond Crystal kosher salt
>   or ¼ teaspoon other kosher salt
>
> 1 tablespoon chopped tender herbs (such as chives, dill, parsley,
>   or tarragon, or a mix)

Break the tofu into pieces in the food processor bowl and process until smooth. Add the vinegar, salt, and herbs. Pulse to mix well.

Store in a covered container in the refrigerator for up to 1 week.

Cashew Cheese

The words "vegan cheese" once elicited shudders, but modern versions made from nuts are a big improvement over the oily plastic sheets of the past. You are welcome to try different nuts—I think peanuts would be great. Although this cheese is simple to put together, you need to think ahead to soak the nuts for at least a few hours.

Nutritional yeast adds a bit of funk to the taste—the umami element of cheese, I guess. A hippie holdover, it is generally available in your local health food store. We bought copious amounts of it online.

We used this on our Vegan Reuben, but it also works as a protein-rich spread for a bagel or a schmear on the side of a salad.

Makes 2 cups

> 2 cups unsalted raw cashews
>
> 4 teaspoons nutritional yeast
>
> ¼ cup fresh lemon juice (about 2 lemons)
>
> 1 clove garlic, peeled and minced
>
> 1 teaspoon Diamond Crystal kosher salt
>   or ½ teaspoon other kosher salt, plus more if needed
>
> 2 turns of a pepper mill

Place the cashews and 3 cups water in a container, cover, and refrigerate for at least 2 hours or up to a day.

Drain the cashews, reserving the water. Place the cashews, nutritional yeast, lemon juice, garlic, salt, and pepper in a food processor. Pulse repeatedly to break the cashews down until they form a coarse, wet meal. Stop the processor and scrape down the sides of the bowl with a spatula.

With the processor on, drizzle in ¼ cup of the reserved water, then process for about 10 seconds. Stop and scrape the bowl again. Process again for 1 to 2 minutes, until smooth and thick, adding an extra tablespoon water if needed. The consistency should be similar to hummus. Taste and pulse in more salt if you think it needs it.

Store in a covered container in the refrigerator for up to a week.

Cream Cheese Schmears

Part of the fun of having a bagel shop is getting to throw around Yiddish words. For instance, "schmear," a delightful word that means "to spread." I used a mixer to paddle heavy cream into our cream cheese (which is mostly cream already) for two reasons: it lightens the texture and renders it spreadable when cold.

You can add just about anything to cream cheese to make it a schmear, so feel free to be creative. Some of my go-to combos follow the basic recipe.

Creamy Cream Cheese Base

Makes 1 cup base

> One 8-ounce package cream cheese, room temperature
> ¼ cup heavy cream

MIXING BY HAND: Place the cream cheese in a large bowl. Beat with a heavy-duty spatula or wooden spoon until very soft. Slowly pour in the cream and continue beating until the base is smooth and free of lumps.

MIXING WITH A STAND MIXER: Place the cream cheese in the bowl of a stand mixer. Using the paddle attachment, beat on medium speed until it is smooth, stopping the mixer and scraping down the bowl a few times. With the mixer on its lowest speed, slowly pour in the cream. Once it has been incorporated, increase the speed to medium. Continue beating until it is a smooth, lump-free base.

MIXING IN A FOOD PROCESSOR: Place the cream cheese in the food processor bowl. Pulse a few times to loosen it. Pour in the cream through the feed chute while processing, until fully incorporated, stopping the machine a few times to scrape down the bowl.

Store in a covered container in the refrigerator for up to a week.

Schmears

HERB: Mince enough fresh herbs such as fennel fronds, dill, parsley, chives, tarragon, and/or scallions to make ¼ to ⅓ cup. Fold these into the base along with 1½ teaspoons dried minced garlic. Makes about 1½ cups.

> *Fresh herbs come in remarkably small and expensive containers at most grocery stores. I find cheaper, large quantities of lovely, fresh herbs at our local Asian market, and recommend trying any international market with a produce section. They are also pretty easy to grow on a sunny window sill or in a container garden, and then you can really go crazy with the green.*

FRUIT: Stir in ¼ cup fruit preserves. We used fig jam regularly, as well as preserves we made out of local fruits in season—berry-rhubarb, raspberry-poblano, and wild plum. Makes about 1¾ cups.

VEGETABLE: Peel, seed, and finely chop one-third of a regular cucumber. Finely chop 1 trimmed radish, ½ peeled carrot, and 1 scallion. Fold these into the base along with up to ½ teaspoon kosher salt. Herbs are good in this one as well. Makes about 2 cups.

HORSERADISH–DILL: Stir in ¼ cup chopped fresh dill, 2 teaspoons prepared horseradish, 1 teaspoon fresh lemon juice, and a few drops of Worcestershire sauce. Makes about 1¾ cups.

MAPLE–BACON: Cook 5 pieces bacon until crisp. Drain, then mince or crumble. Stir into the base with 2 tablespoons maple syrup and ½ teaspoon chopped fresh thyme leaves or a pinch of dried thyme. Makes about 1¾ cups.

PIMENTO CHEESE: Roast, peel, seed, and dice 1 red bell pepper and 1 green bell pepper. Fold these into the base along with 8 ounces (2 cups) grated cheddar cheese, 1½ tablespoons mayonnaise, a pinch each of sugar and cayenne pepper, and a dash of hot sauce (I recommend Cholula). Makes about 2½ cups.

REUBEN: Fold in 1 tablespoon Pickled Mustard Seeds (page 113), ½ cup shredded pastrami bits, ½ cup grated Gruyère or Swiss cheese, 1 tablespoon Dijon mustard, and 1 minced shallot. Makes about 2½ cups.

SMOKED SALMON: Fold in 4 ounces hot-smoked or kippered salmon, skin removed, crumbled (about ¾ cup). Makes about 2 generous cups.

In Jewish food, there are two basic versions of salmon. One is lox, which has been brined or cured and smoked at a cool temperature; this yields the Nova lox we are used to seeing draped on a bagel. The other is hot–smoked salmon (also called baked or kippered salmon) that has been cured, then smoked for a shorter time at a higher temperature; this yields a cooked texture and easily flaked salmon.

Chopped Liver

This is actually a chicken liver mousse that I like more than traditional chopped liver. The original recipe came from a fellow chef in Fargo, Mason Lewis. We adapted it for our use by taking out the fancy ingredients—truffles, port, Madeira, brandy—but keeping the enormous quantity of butter, which is emulsified into the mousse.

This is a recipe that even liver haters like, a gateway drug to the pleasures of pâté. It is great with bread and an assortment of pickles (of course), on a banh mi sandwich, or just with a few crackers.

Makes 1½ cups

> 1 shallot (about 1 ounce), ends trimmed, peeled, and halved lengthwise
> 5 tablespoons apple cider vinegar
> 2 tablespoons + 1½ teaspoons granulated sugar
> 13 tablespoons (1½ sticks + 1 tablespoon) unsalted butter
> 1 large egg
> 2 large yolks
> 8 ounces chicken livers
> ⅛ teaspoon TCM (tinted curing mix) or pink curing salt (optional)*

> *This will keep the pâté a pleasant pink color.*

Place the shallot halves cut side down on the cutting board. Slice them from root to stem end, into long, thin matchstick pieces. Place in a saucepan and add the vinegar and sugar. Cook over medium heat until the liquid has reduced by two-thirds and is quite syrupy (about 5 minutes). Set aside.

Melt the butter in a saucepan over low heat or in a microwave-safe bowl in the microwave. Set aside to cool, but don't let it solidify.

Beat the egg and yolks in a medium bowl until blended. Fold in the chicken livers.

Place the shallot and its syrup and the chicken liver mixture in the blender jar. While the blender is on, slowly pour in the still-liquid butter. Once everything is well mixed

and emulsified, pour the mixture through a
medium-mesh strainer into another bowl. (You
want to strain out anything that would keep the
end product from being completely smooth.)
You may need to use a ladle or the back of a
spoon to press the mixture through the sieve. If using the curing salt, stir it in until
fully dissolved and mixed through.

Preheat the oven to 250°F. Choose the container(s) you'll cook the mousse in—
I usually use three 5-ounce individual ramekins, but you could use a pint-sized pâté
mold, or an oven-safe bowl. Once you have decided on the cooking container(s),
turn it/them upside down on a sheet of parchment paper and trace around the
edge(s). Cut out the tracing(s) to create fitted lids that you will press down on the
surface of the mousse.

Bring a kettle of water to a boil. Find a 2- to 3-inch-deep casserole dish or roasting
pan that will comfortably fit the cooking container(s) you chose.

Pour the mousse into the cooking container(s), top with the parchment lid(s), and
place in the casserole. Place the casserole on the middle shelf of the oven. Pour
the boiled water into the casserole around the container(s), adding enough water to
reach halfway up the sides of the container(s). Cover the casserole with foil. Bake
for 30 to 40 minutes until the mousse is set but with a little jiggle in the center (like
a crème brûlée) and reaches 138°F. To check, remove the foil and stick an instant-
read thermometer halfway down into the center of the mousse. If it has not reached
138°F, replace the foil and bake for another 5 minutes before checking again.

Using a large offset spatula or tongs, carefully remove the cooking container(s) from
the water bath and transfer them to a wire cooling rack on the counter. Let cool to
room temperature, still covered by the parchment. (For safety, let the casserole of
water cool in the oven before you remove it.)

Cover tightly with plastic wrap and refrigerate for up to 3 days. Or freeze for up to
a month and defrost in the refrigerator for a day. Serve in the ramekin.

Labne

Labne is a yogurt cheese of Middle Eastern origins. It is a tarter and lighter option than cream cheese, and easy to make at home. You want to start with real yogurt, not chemicals that taste like yogurt; look for a brand that has understandable and few ingredients—for example, just milk and live, active cultures. To serve, top it with za'atar, fresh herbs, chile flakes (I'm currently in love with urfa biber flakes from Turkey), and/or minced scallions, and a splash of extra virgin olive oil.

We liked to pair Labne with Hummus or Zhug, but use it wherever you would use a fresh or creamy cheese. Save the liquid whey that drains off and use it for marinating or in dressings and sauces—like you would buttermilk.

Makes about 1½ cups

> 2 cups plain Greek-style yogurt*
> 1 teaspoon Diamond Crystal kosher salt or ½ teaspoon other kosher salt
> 1 tablespoon extra virgin olive oil

> *The fat content is up to you; I prefer full-fat for roundness of flavor.*

Mix the yogurt, salt, and olive oil with a spatula in a medium bowl. Set a fine-mesh strainer over a bowl and pour in the yogurt mixture. If you don't have a fine-mesh strainer, layer two 12 × 12-inch squares of cheesecloth. Spoon the yogurt mixture into the center and gather up the corners, hobo-pack style. Wrap the gathered corners with twine, and tie the twine around a pencil or butter knife. Balance the pencil across the top of a deep container to suspend the cheesecloth pack so the whey can drain off.

Place yogurt mixture in the refrigerator and let drain for at least a day, or up to 3 days.

Store in a covered container in the refrigerator for up to 1 week.

MARINATED LABNE BALLS: For a tasty, firmer variation, drain the yogurt longer—2 to 3 days—until it has the texture of a fresh goat cheese. Roll into little balls and submerge them in good-quality extra virgin olive oil. You can roll the balls in herbs before adding them to the oil—za'atar, minced fresh or crumbled dried mint, Everything Bagel Mix (page 22), whatever sounds good to you. Store in the refrigerator for up to 2 weeks.

Quick Pickles

When I was the chef at the Hotel Donaldson, I made a grand plan with our main farmer, the polymath Kimberly Hess, to pickle hundreds of beets so that we would have them through the winter. We canned them and put them in our pantry—shelf after shelf of colorful jars. A week later, the health inspector stopped by and informed us that we would have to throw out all 20 gallons of pickles as we were not a certified canning kitchen and we hadn't had the pH of the pickles lab tested. I took my chances and brought dozens of jars of them home, but at least 50 pounds went in the garbage.

Since that imbroglio, I like to keep it simple and quick-pickle instead—that is, make a brine (a salt- or acid-based solution) and throw it over vegetables and fruits. Obviously, these are not shelf stable and must be kept refrigerated. Most of these pickles are ready in a few days, and some can last for up to a month. At BernBaum's, we made at least 100 pounds of assorted pickles weekly—even more in the summer when overtaken by garden bounty.

Sweet Brine Pickles

I found the original of this recipe in Marcus Samuelsson's glorious cookbook, *Aquavit: And the New Scandinavian Cuisine*. I adapted his brine to use for a variety of pickled condiments. It is also lovely with fresh summer rhubarb and one of our best creations, summer melon and hot peppers; see the variations that follow.

Makes about 2 cups brine, enough for about 4 to 6 cups of pickled vegetables

½ teaspoon coriander seeds*

½ teaspoon cumin seeds

1 small dried chile (your choice)

1 allspice berry or 3 peppercorns

½ cup apple cider vinegar

1 cup granulated sugar

4 cups cleaned, trimmed, and chopped vegetables or fruit, peeled if necessary**

Instead of the coriander, cumin, chile, and allspice or peppercorns, you can use 1½ teaspoons pickling spice.

**Use any vegetable or fruit that you want. See the variations that follow for some suggestions.*

Place a dry medium saucepan over medium heat. Once the pan is warm, about 45 seconds, add the coriander, cumin, chile, and allspice or peppercorns (or pickling spice) and toast until fragrant, about a minute.

Add the vinegar and sugar. Stir to help the sugar dissolve. Bring to a simmer and cook until the sugar is fully dissolved, about 5 minutes. Remove from the heat and stir in 1½ cups water.

Pack the vegetables into a clean 1-quart jar or a heavy-duty plastic or stainless steel container. Pour the brine over, taking care to submerge the vegetables in the brine. The vegetables will shrink in the brine as they pickle, so you need just enough brine to get almost to the top of the vegetables. Cover tightly and refrigerate.

Most pickles should taste good after a day in the brine. They will keep for a month (or more), refrigerated.

FENNEL–CUCUMBER: Thinly slice 1⅓ English cucumbers and 1 trimmed fennel bulb crosswise on a mandoline or with a sharp knife if you are feeling confident.

RED ONION: Trim and peel 2 or 3 small red onions, or 1 to 1½ jumbo onions (about 1 pound total). Slice the onions into ⅛-inch-thick rings or half-moons with a mandoline or sharp knife.

MELON AND HOT PEPPER: Peel, seed, and cube 1 garden-fresh melon (we used Charentais, which are small, but if you have more melon than you need, have a snack). Slice 1 or 2 chiles (your choice) into thin rounds; deseed if you would like the pickle to be milder.

RHUBARB: Trim the leaves off 3 or 4 stalks. Thinly slice the stalks on the bias.

Dill Brine Pickles

This brine is amazing on Brussels sprouts, garlic scapes, green beans, and asparagus.

Makes about 2 cups brine, enough for 1 quart of vegetables

> 4 cups cleaned, trimmed, peeled and large-diced
> (if necessary) vegetables
>
> 1 clove garlic, unpeeled, smashed with the side of
> a knife blade
>
> 1 sprig fresh dill or ¼ teaspoon dill seeds
>
> ½ teaspoon celery seeds (optional)
>
> 1½ cups distilled white vinegar
>
> ¼ cup Diamond Crystal kosher salt
> or 2 tablespoons other kosher salt

Pack the vegetables into a clean 1-quart container—a glass canning jar is perfect, but a heavy-duty plastic or stainless steel container can work as well. Add the garlic and dill, and the celery seeds (if using).

Bring the vinegar, salt, and ½ cup water to a boil in a small saucepan. Reduce the heat to a simmer and cook for 5 minutes, until salt is fully dissolved. Pour over the vegetables and let cool to room temperature. Cover the container and refrigerate for at least 2 days before serving. These will last for a month, refrigerated.

Pickled Apples

Adapted from the *Momofuku* cookbook, we used this brine to pickle thinly sliced apples, which we added to Smoked Trout Salad and Chicken Walnut Salad sandwiches as well as salads, and served on the side of our chopped liver plate.

To get uniformly lovely slices of apple, core out the center of the apple and use a Japanese-style mandoline (aka Benriner), a bargain tool that ups your salad and garnishing game.

Makes about 1½ cups brine, enough for 2 apples or 2 to 3 cups vegetables or other fruit

⅓ cup granulated sugar

2 teaspoons Diamond Crystal kosher salt or 1 teaspoon other kosher salt

½ cup rice vinegar

2 apples (your choice), cored and thinly sliced*

Substitute 2 to 3 cups vegetables or fruits of your choice, cleaned, peeled if necessary, trimmed, and sliced or diced.

Bring 1 cup water to a boil in a small saucepan. Remove from the heat and add the sugar and salt. Stir to dissolve the sugar and salt, then add the vinegar. Cool to room temperature.

Place the apple slices in a clean glass jar and pour the brine over to submerge them. Cover and refrigerate. These will last for 4 days refrigerated before starting to brown.

Bread and Butter Pickles

This is a recipe from former BernBaum's chef Paul Perez, which we used as a garnish on our sandwich plates. Every morning, I would place a healthy amount of these atop some schmear on a rye bread butt. Pickle toast is the best breakfast.

Make 1 quart

> 1 pound cucumbers (4 Persian, 1¼ seedless English,
>   or 2 peeled and seeded standard garden cucumbers)
>
> ½ small onion (halved from root to stem), peeled, ends trimmed
>
> 1 large sprig fresh dill, pulled into smaller sprigs
>
> 1 teaspoon coriander seeds or ½ teaspoon ground coriander
>
> 1 teaspoon brown or yellow mustard seeds
>
> ¼ teaspoon celery seeds
>
> ⅛ teaspoon ground turmeric
>
> ¾ cup apple cider vinegar
>
> ⅓ cup granulated sugar
>
> 2 teaspoons Diamond Crystal kosher salt or 1 teaspoon other kosher salt

Slice the cucumbers about ¼ inch thick and place in a large bowl. Place the onion cut side down on the cutting board and slice them from stem to root end to get ¼-inch-wide strips. Add the onion strips and dill to the cucumbers and toss to combine. Transfer them to the clean container that will be their home in the refrigerator—a 1-quart glass canning jar, heavy-duty plastic container, or stainless steel container. Set aside.

Place a dry medium saucepan over medium heat. Once the pan is warm, about 45 seconds, add the coriander, mustard, and celery seeds and toast until fragrant, 1 to 2 minutes. Add the turmeric, vinegar, ½ cup + 1 tablespoon water, the sugar, and the salt. Bring to a boil, stirring to dissolve the sugar and salt. Pour the hot brine over the cucumbers and onions. (If the brine doesn't cover the pickles, don't worry. The cucumbers will shrink into the brine.) Let cool. When close to room temperature, place in the refrigerator.

After the pickles are chilled, cover the container. The pickles will be ready to serve after a day or two, and will last for up to a month, refrigerated.

Dill
1·31
Dill
1·31
Dill
1·31
Dill
1·31
PRO
1·29
PRO
1·29

Grandma Gladys's Carrot Relish

My Grandma Gladys lived to 105 and spent a longer lifetime cooking for others than most. The eldest of 10 children—pulled out of school at age 13 to take care of the younger ones—and later the mother of 8, she knew how to feed a crowd. And she kept feeding us into her nineties. My dad remembers that she would use a hand-cranked grinder to make a large batch of her carrot relish; he was pressed into service with it from a young age. He enjoyed it, showing his aptitude for kitchen labor early.

If you have a food processor with a shredding disk, this is an easy recipe. Otherwise, get yourself ready for a small workout, using a box grater to shred the carrot, onion, and cucumber.

My grandma would can her carrot relish in the traditional way (i.e., making an enormous batch with garden produce each summer and putting up the jars in a pantry for use in the winter), but I don't. She also served it as a side with supper, like a typical Midwestern pickle eater. We used it as a condiment. I like it on sandwiches, and it's a perfect accompaniment to a roast of any kind.

Makes 2 to 3 cups

- 2 carrots (about 10 ounces total), root and stem ends trimmed, peeled
- 1 medium onion, peeled, root and stem ends trimmed
- 1 cucumber, peeled and seeded (about 6 ounces)
- 2 teaspoons Diamond Crystal kosher salt or 1 teaspoon other kosher salt
- ⅓ cup apple cider vinegar
- ⅓ cup granulated sugar
- ¼ teaspoon celery seeds
- ½ teaspoon mustard seeds

Grate the carrots, onion, and cucumber in a food processor with a shredding disk, then transfer the vegetables and any accumulated liquid to a large bowl. Or grate them on the large holes of a box grater directly into a large bowl. Sprinkle with the salt and mix well with a sturdy wooden spoon or your gloved hands.

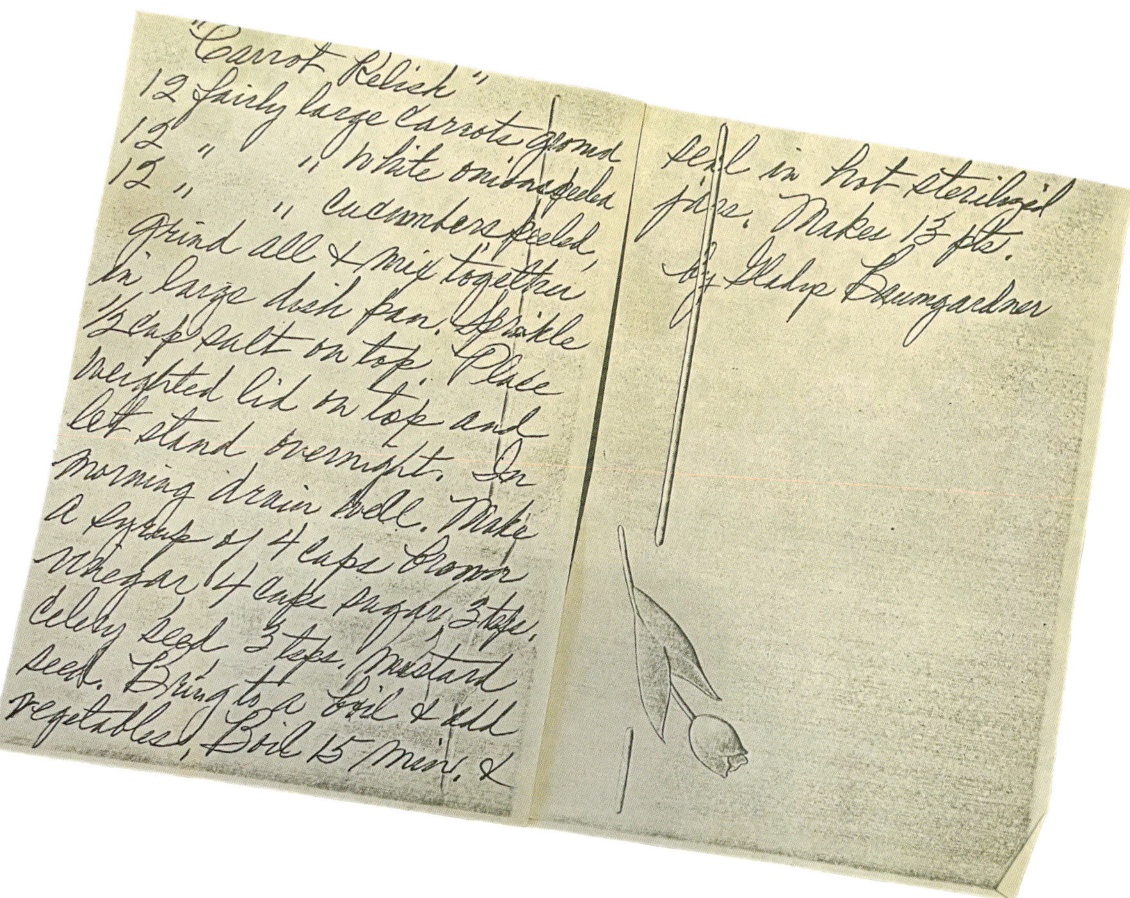

Pack the vegetables into a 1-quart bowl or heavy-duty plastic container. Press plastic wrap directly onto the top of the vegetables and cover with a slightly smaller diameter lid or plate (to weight the vegetables under the brine). Let stand in the refrigerator overnight.

The next morning, drain off the liquid and mix the vegetables well.

Bring the vinegar, sugar, and celery and mustard seeds to a boil in a medium saucepan. Add the vegetables and bring to a simmer. Lower the heat to maintain the simmer for 5 minutes. Pour into a clean 1-quart glass jar or clean plastic container and let cool to room temperature. Cover and refrigerate. The relish should last for at least a month in the refrigerator.

Carrot–Horseradish Relish

Years ago, we did a special Passover dinner with cookbook author, restaurateur, and Food Network cutie–patootie Molly Yeh, and we had the last minute help (miracle of miracles) of the longtime pastry chef at Gramercy Tavern, Nancy Olson. We used this condiment, inspired by Jeffrey Yoskowitz and Liz Alpern's book, *The Gefilte Manifesto: New Recipes for Old World Jewish Foods*, with housemade gefilte fish, and it was a blockbuster. After the dinner, we added the relish to a smoked brisket and lox schmear sandwich. I like it with the Bacon, Egg, and Cheese bagel. There can never be too many pickles.

Makes 1½ to 2 cups

> 2 or 3 carrots (about ½ pound), peeled, root and stem ends trimmed
> 2 tablespoons prepared horseradish
> 4 teaspoons granulated sugar
> 4 teaspoons distilled white vinegar
> Grated zest and juice of 1 lemon
> ⅛ teaspoon Diamond Crystal kosher salt or 1 pinch other kosher salt

Grate the carrots on the large holes of a box grater into a large heatproof bowl. (You can also use a food processor fitted with a shredding disk, and transfer the carrots to a bowl.) Add the horseradish and mix well with your gloved hands or a sturdy wooden spoon.

Bring the sugar, vinegar, and ⅓ cup water to a boil in a small saucepan. Simmer until the sugar is dissolved. Remove from the heat and add the lemon zest and juice and the salt. Mix into the carrot-horseradish mixture.

Pack the relish into a clean 2-cup glass jar or heavy-duty plastic container. Cover with plastic, pressing it down onto the surface of the relish. Cover with a lid or more plastic wrap and refrigerate.

This will last, refrigerated, for up to a month.

Nancy Olson, Andrea, and Molly Yeh in the BernBaum's kitchen.

Fermented Sauerkraut

Brett's parents gave me the crock his Grandmother Mary used to make pickles. It sat unused in our home kitchen for a year until former BernBaum's chef Grady Ryan willed it into use for some pretty great sauerkraut. Here is Grady's recipe, with some input from his parents and assorted older Germans.

While this is a simple recipe, it is necessary to make sure that all of your surfaces, containers, and utensils (including your hands) are clean. The bacteria fermenting the cabbage should keep out any bad microbes, but it is still a good idea to follow all food safety precautions.

Makes about 6 to 8 cups

> 1 head cabbage* (about 1¾ pounds)
>
> ½ small onion, peeled, root and stem ends trimmed
>
> 1 teaspoon caraway seeds
>
> 2 tablespoons + 1 teaspoon Diamond Crystal kosher salt
>   or 3½ teaspoons other kosher salt

**We generally used green cabbage, but red works as well.*

To be exact, you will need to weigh the cabbage after it is trimmed, cored, and shredded in order to calculate the amount of salt needed. You need salt equal to 2.5% of the weight of the prepped cabbage. A cabbage weighing approximately 1¾ pounds before trimming should give you a little under 1½ pounds trimmed. We averaged the amounts in order to save you from having to do math. If your cabbage weighs more or less, weigh the bowl you'll be mixing it in before you add the cabbage, then tare the scale to get the exact weight of the cabbage.

Take the loose outer leaves off of the cabbage. Cut the head in half through the core, then cut the core out by making V-cuts all around it into each half. Place one half cut side down on a cutting board and slice it crosswise to create very thin ribbons. (You can also use your trusty mandoline, or a food processor with a slicing disk. Cut the halves to fit first.) Repeat with the other half. Place the cabbage in a large bowl.

recipe continues

Place the cut side of the onion down on the cutting board and slice it into thin strips from root to stem end. Add to the cabbage. Add the caraway and salt. Mix thoroughly with gloved hands, massaging the salt into the cabbage well; this is what will cause the cabbage to lose water and create the brine of the sauerkraut. Pack the salted cabbage into a clean cylindrical or rectangular crock or other container that is more tall than wide.

To keep out contaminants, place a layer of plastic wrap atop the cabbage so that it fully covers the surface and tamp it down so that there is no air between the kraut and the plastic wrap. Fill a gallon-size resealable plastic bag two-thirds full with water and seal it. Place this bag atop the plastic wrap. If it doesn't cover all the plastic, add another bag of water.

Cover the crock with its lid and then use plastic wrap to tightly cover the lid and the crock. Place it in a cool and dry environment (70°F or lower, but not refrigerated), outside of direct light, for at least a week, preferably 1 to 2 weeks. Check it after 1 week. The sauerkraut will taste more pickled and sour the longer it ferments. If you check your kraut and discover fruit flies or mold, or if the cabbage appears purple or brown, discard and start over.

Once the sauerkraut is as fermented as you want it, transfer it into a clean 2-quart heavy-duty plastic container or several smaller containers. Make sure the sauerkraut is submerged in brine. Cover the container(s) and store in the refrigerator for up to 1 month.

Kraut Tzatziki

We improvised this to go with our Chicken Schnitzel plate. It was a fabulous complement to the lingonberries and sweet pickles. Pair this with any rich, fatty meat dish.

Makes 2 cups

> 1 cup plain Greek yogurt
>
> ¾ cup Fermented Sauerkraut (page 89), drained and chopped
>
> 1 tablespoon chopped cornichons*
>
> 1 teaspoon minced fresh dill
>
> ½ teaspoon Hawaij Spice Mix (page 92)
>
> *Cornichons are tiny, tart, crunchy French dill pickles. If you don't have any, substitute minced regular dill pickles (even the ones on page 80!).*

Mix the yogurt, sauerkraut, cornichons, dill, and spice mix together in a bowl. Cover and refrigerate for at least 1 day for it to develop flavor and a beautiful turmeric-gold color. This lasts up to 1 week in the refrigerator.

Hawaij Spice Mix

We used this Yemeni spice blend in the Kraut Tzatziki and our Vegetarian Matzo Ball Soup.

This is perfect in any number of soups and stews—even coffee—to add a spicy and warm note to the dish. If you become addicted, this recipe is easily doubled or tripled.

Makes a scant ¼ cup

> 2 tablespoons cumin seeds or 4½ teaspoons ground cumin
>
> 1 tablespoon black peppercorns or 2½ teaspoons ground black pepper
>
> 1 teaspoon coriander seeds or ¾ teaspoon ground coriander
>
> ¼ teaspoon cardamom seeds (from 2 green cardamom pods) or ¼ teaspoon ground cardamom
>
> 1 tablespoon ground turmeric

Heat a dry sauté pan over medium heat for about 45 seconds. If using whole spices, add the cumin, peppercorns, coriander, and cardamom and toast until fragrant, about 2 minutes, stirring from time to time. If using ground spices, toast the cumin, pepper, coriander, and cardamom for 30 seconds to a minute. Pay attention, as the spices can go from fragrant to burned quickly. Remove from the heat, pour onto a plate, and let cool.

Blend to a powder in a spice grinder, clean coffee grinder, or with a mortar and pestle. Pour into a bowl. Add the turmeric and mix well with a whisk.

Store in a clean, dry covered container at room temperature for up to 3 months.

Krautsalat

Krautsalat literally means "cabbage salad" in German. In this case, it is a marinated cabbage slaw that makes a great side dish for barbecue (something decidedly not part of BernBaum's repertoire, although we heartily support it) as well as a pickled part of a sandwich. We used it on the Vegan Reuben and Turkey Pastrami sandwiches.

Makes 2 cups

> ¼ head of a large (3 lb+) cabbage or ½ head of a small (1–2 lb) cabbage to yield about 10 to 12 ounces, outer leaves discarded, cored
>
> 1 tablespoon + ½ teaspoon Diamond Crystal kosher salt or 1¾ teaspoons other kosher salt
>
> 1 small carrot, peeled, root and stem ends trimmed, shredded
>
> ½ small shallot, peeled and minced
>
> 2 teaspoons minced fresh herbs (like parsley, dill, chives, tarragon)
>
> 1 tablespoon white wine vinegar, apple cider vinegar, or red wine vinegar
>
> 1 tablespoon fresh lemon juice
>
> 2 turns of a pepper mill
>
> 2 tablespoons canola oil

Slice the cabbage as thinly as possible, either by hand on a cutting board with a sharp knife or in a food processor with a slicing disk. (If using a food processor, cut the wedge into thirds so it will fit through the feed chute.) Place the cabbage in a large heatproof bowl.

Bring 4 cups water and 1 tablespoon Diamond Crystal salt or 1½ teaspoons other kosher salt to a boil in a medium saucepan. Remove from heat and pour over the cabbage, ensuring that all the cabbage is submerged in the water. (Add more water if it doesn't cover.) Let sit until the water is cool, between 30 and 60 minutes.

recipe continues

The Vegan Reuben, ready for its close-up.

Drain the cabbage in a colander set in the sink. Press down on top of the cabbage with a plate that is slightly narrower than the colander to press out as much water as possible.

Put the cabbage in a clean large bowl. Add the carrot, shallot, and herbs. In a small bowl, combine the vinegar, lemon juice, ½ teaspoon Diamond Crystal or ¼ teaspoon other kosher salt, and the pepper. Slowly whisk in the oil until blended. Pour this vinaigrette over the cabbage and toss to coat the vegetables evenly. Taste for salt, adding more if needed. Transfer the krautsalat to a covered container and refrigerate for at least 12 hours before serving. (It gets better throughout its first few days as the cabbage completely absorbs the vinaigrette.)

This will keep for up to a week, refrigerated.

Gravlax

Gravlax is a cured fish—kind of a pickle—that is generally made with salmon although we liked to use Arctic char. We served it on our Iceland Bagel Plate with Fennel-Cucumber Pickles, Pickled Red Onion, capers, and schmear of chèvre (soft goat cheese).

Gravlax is lovely on rye toast with a sweet mustard sauce as a before-meal bite—or maybe as an entree if you enjoy your cured fish. The lovely thing about gravlax is that a little goes a long way. A half-pound of fish can give you an hors d'oeuvre for 8 people.

Curing is an ancient way of preserving food with salt, sugar, and spices. Because the fish isn't cooked, it is important to buy the freshest and highest-quality fish possible and treat it carefully. This is not a recipe to make for a pregnant friend.

Serves 8 as an hors d'oeuvre

1 teaspoon coriander seeds, crushed*

1 teaspoon cardamom seeds, crushed*

6 tablespoons kosher salt (any brand)

¾ cup granulated sugar

8 ounces skin-on Arctic char or salmon fillet, pin bones out

¼ cup chopped mixed fresh dill and fennel fronds

To crush the seeds, place them in a heavy-duty resealable plastic bag and hit them with a mallet or sauté pan. You can also pulse them in a spice grinder or blender.

Heat a sauté pan over medium-high heat for about 45 seconds. Add the coriander and cardamom and toast them for about 1 minute, stirring frequently to keep them from burning. Add the salt and continue to stir until fragrant. Transfer to a small bowl and let cool.

recipe continues

Add the sugar and mix well. If not using immediately, store in a covered container for up to a month. Makes 1 scant cup of cure.

Score the skin of the fillet a few times, making sure not to cut too deeply—just through the skin. Spread a good layer of cure in a casserole dish or loaf pan that comfortably fits the fish. Place the fillet skin side down on the cure. Spread the remaining cure on to cover the fish so you don't see the flesh. Top with the dill and fennel fronds. Place a layer of plastic wrap directly on top of the fish, cover with a similarly sized container, and weight that down with a few cans. Refrigerate for at least 24 hours, and up to 48 hours. (You don't want the fish to dry out, and anything longer than that will make it tough and jerky-like.)

Rinse the gravlax thoroughly under cold running water and pat dry. To serve, slice the gravlax off the skin into thin, almost transparent pieces with a sharp, thin-bladed knife, holding the knife at about a 45 degree angle. (You can use a sharper angle, less than 45 degrees, for wider slices or more than 45 degrees for narrower ones— whatever you prefer.)

If you aren't serving the gravlax immediately, double-wrap it in plastic and refrigerate for up to 2 days or freeze for up to a month. Defrost in the refrigerator before serving.

Hot–Smoked Salmon

We started smoking on a backyard Big Green Egg, which is a fantastic smoker—especially in the winter, when subzero temps keep the fire low but the smoke going. (My best temperature was about 250°F.) We then bought an entry–level commercial smoker, which did the job most of the time. It allowed us to smoke pastrami and lots(!) of carrots for our vegan Smoked Carrot Lox, and do our own Hot–Smoked Salmon, as well as the random spice or vegetable experiment.

We used this in our Smoked Salmon schmear and also sold it by the quarter–pound, but the cure works for chicken, duck, and all sorts of different meats—whether you are smoking them or not. Curing the meat allows it to retain moisture during cooking (the same principle as brining) and is a good fix for boneless, skinless anything.

This is great with a scoop of the Herb Schmear (page 72) and a bunch of Bagel Chips (page 24). Note that it takes at least 3 days, start to finish.

Makes a generous pound of smoked salmon (4 to 6 servings at least)

> 1 cup light brown sugar
>
> ¼ cup Hungarian or Spanish sweet paprika
>
> ½ cup + 2 tablespoons Diamond Crystal kosher salt
>   or 5 tablespoons other kosher salt
>
> 1 to 1½ pounds salmon fillet* in one piece, pin bones out,
>   skin on or off (your choice)
>
> Nonstick baking spray
>
> **Preferably sustainably raised like Verlasso (farmed), organic Scottish, or wild caught.*

Mix the brown sugar, paprika, and salt to make the cure. You can store it for up to a year in a covered container in your pantry; you'll have about 1½ cups.

Place the salmon skin side down on a baking sheet. With your gloved hand or the back of a spoon, spread the fish with a thick layer of the cure so that it reaches all surfaces of the flesh, including sides. Refrigerate uncovered for at least 24 hours or up to 2 days.

On the second day, rinse the salmon under cold running water. Dry as thoroughly as possible with paper towels. Wash and dry the baking sheet and return the salmon to it, skin side down. Refrigerate uncovered in the refrigerator to dry for 1 to 2 days. (Drying the flesh allows it to retain more of the smoke later.)

On the third day, preheat your smoker or grill, following the manufacturer's directions. Meanwhile, soak 2 cups wood chips, chunks, or pellets in water for at least 15 minutes, then drain well. (If you're using a stovetop smoker, use about 2 tablespoons unsoaked wood chips.) Add the wood to the smoker according to directions. Place the grate at least 8 inches above the heat source and spray it with nonstick cooking spray. Place the salmon fillet atop the grate, skin side down, and close the cover. Monitor and control the temperature to keep it as low as possible while still maintaining the smoke. It should take 15 to 20 minutes to fully cook and smoke the salmon, depending on the temperature.

We used applewood, but oak and hickory are also great!

When the salmon reaches 130°F (check with an instant-read thermometer), remove it from the smoker and place on a clean baking sheet or platter. Let it cool at room temperature for at least 30 minutes. Wrap and refrigerate until fully cooled before using.

Store covered in the refrigerator for up to 4 days. You can also double-wrap it in plastic and freeze for up to a month. Defrost in the refrigerator before serving.

Smoked Carrot Lox

This recipe came about because we were looking for a vegan stand-in for smoked meat and fish. The carrots look lovely when shaved into thin ribbons and add a substantial smoky flavor to any dish.

While this doesn't taste like salmon, the sweetness of the carrots, the smoke, and the zing of the rice vinegar create an equally delicious plate. You can also use this recipe to smoke other vegetables. Most root vegetables handle the recipe exactly. More delicate items such as mushrooms don't take as long to smoke.

Makes 3 cups; serves 4 to 6

> Kosher salt (any brand)
>
> 1 pound carrots, stems trimmed, scrubbed well
>
> 2 tablespoons rice vinegar

Sprinkle a thin layer of salt in a metal baking pan or flameproof casserole dish that will fit in your smoker or grill. Place a layer of carrots atop the salt, then sprinkle them with a thin layer of salt. If the carrots don't all fit in one layer, continue layering carrots, salt, carrots, and salt.

Prepare your smoker or grill to 275°F. Place the pan of carrots on the grill and close the cover. If the carrots are smaller (¾-inch or less diameter on the stem end), smoke for 30 to 45 minutes, checking every 15 minutes. If the carrots are larger, smoke for 1 to 1½ hours, replenishing the wood if necessary. The carrots should taste very smoky, but still be firm and not fully cooked. Remove from the smoker and cool to room temperature. (The salt will have dissolved in the smoking process.)

Slice the carrots very thin along their length with a mandoline (or a vegetable peeler). Toss the carrot slices in a bowl with the vinegar until coated. Store in a covered container or heavy-duty resealable plastic bag in the refrigerator for up to 5 days.

The safest way to shave the carrots is with a really good peeler. The carrots might be a little thin, but you won't have sliced your hand off. We sliced them on a meat slicer or used a mandoline. In those cases, it was important to use a cut-proof glove, as it is remarkably easy to wound yourself. If you don't own a cut-proof glove, I have found that a double layer of regular disposable gloves provides some protection.

Sauces and Other Condiments

Freed from the long arm of formal French sauces, our dressings and condiments relied more on a mildly tart creaminess, an unctuous herby zhug, or the sharpness of chiles and mustard. These are sauces that deliver more flavor with less labor at the stove, and will elevate the simplest of dishes.

Zhug

A sometimes fiery condiment of Israeli–Yemeni descent, zhug is addictive.
(I mispronounce it as *jhoog*, but have heard *tsoog* and *jhug*—short *u*—spoken.) Alyssa
Anne Miller, friend and customer, calls it "green love." Our green love is quite tame—
I guess it's the Nordic–German version. Feel free to amp up the chile flakes or add fresh
hot chiles. We hand-chopped the cilantro to make our own loose herb sauce.

Makes 1½ to 2 cups

> 1 bunch cilantro, washed, dried, and trimmed of any ugly spots
>
> 1 clove garlic, peeled
>
> 1 teaspoon Diamond Crystal kosher salt or ½ teaspoon other kosher salt
>
> ½ teaspoon chile flakes
>
> Pinch of urfa biber flakes (optional, but very tasty)
>
> ½ teaspoon cumin seeds, toasted and ground,
>   or ⅓ teaspoon ground cumin
>
> ¼ teaspoon caraway seeds, toasted and ground,
>   or scant ¼ teaspoon ground caraway,
>
> About 1½ cups extra virgin olive oil

*To toast or not to toast? At BernBaum's, we toasted the cumin and caraway seeds
in a dry skillet over medium heat until fragrant—a minute or so—then ground them
in a spice grinder. However, you can buy ground cumin and caraway and toast
them lightly—they will toast much more quickly than the whole seeds, in only about
20 to 30 seconds. Or you can choose not to toast at all. I really like the added
complexity of toasted spices, but the zhug will still taste great without toasting.*

Slice the cilantro crosswise, very thin, including the tender stems. Place the cilantro
in a bowl. (Do not rough-chop tender herbs, going back and forth over them, as that
will bruise and blacken the herbs.)

Mince the garlic. To get it as pureed as possible, sprinkle it with a pinch of the salt
and use the side of your knife to rub it into the cutting board. Add it to the cilantro.
Stir in the chile flakes, urfa biber (if using), caraway, and cumin. Stir in the olive oil—
you will want enough oil to cover the herbs by at least ½ an inch, which also keeps
them bright and green.

If not serving immediately, store in a covered container for up to 6 days in the
refrigerator.

Black Garlic Tehina

Black garlic is an aged and fermented garlic that adds a particular, almost Worcestershire edge to this sauce. You can buy it through specialty food purveyors or online.

If you want a thick plate schmear, use a food processor to make this umami–rich accompaniment to Whipped Tofu (page 69). For use as a dressing or thinner sauce, use a whisk or blender. (This may be counterintuitive, but it works.)

Makes about 2 cups

1 head black garlic, cloves separated and peeled

½ cup fresh lemon juice (2½ to 3 lemons)

1 cup tehina (aka tahini—ground sesame paste)

Kosher salt

Balsamic vinegar

If you wonder why we use "tehina" here, it is the Hebrew word for sesame seed paste, whereas "tahini" is Greek. I use both, in keeping with my Libra personality.

USING A FOOD PROCESSOR OR BLENDER: Place the black garlic, lemon juice, and tahini in the food processor bowl or blender jar. Start processing while you slowly add ½ cup water. When it is almost your preferred consistency, season to taste with salt and balsamic vinegar before turning off the machine.

USING A WHISK: Place the black garlic in a medium bowl. Mash it with a sturdy whisk until it is smooth. Add the lemon juice and tahini and whisk until blended. Gradually whisk in ½ cup water until it's your preferred consistency. Season to taste with salt and vinegar.

Transfer to a covered container and refrigerate for up to a week.

Amy Rice, BernBaum's sanity-saving first employee, in action (as always).

German Mustard

We devised this concoction to go on our Brisket Sandwich. Customers often asked to buy a jar.

Slather it on sandwiches, or serve alongside pâté, charcuterie plates, or a hunk of roasted meat. I like it on toast for my morning pickle–palooza.

Makes 2 to 2½ cups

1 shallot, both ends trimmed, peeled

2 cloves garlic, peeled

2 tablespoons minced fennel fronds or fresh dill

1 teaspoon paprika (preferably Hungarian, but any sweet paprika works)

1¼ cups Gulden's or other prepared brown mustard

3 tablespoons whole-grain mustard (preferably Dijon)

1 teaspoon molasses*

3 tablespoons mayonnaise

1½ tablespoons honey

2 teaspoons apple cider vinegar

**I don't recommend using blackstrap molasses; it has too intense a flavor.*

Mince the shallot and garlic together with the fennel fronds. Transfer them to a 1-quart or larger mixing bowl. Add the paprika, brown and whole-grain mustards, molasses, mayo, honey, and vinegar. Mix well with a whisk.

Store in a covered container in the refrigerator for up to a week; the flavors will meld and mellow with time.

Fresh Pepper Harissa

Harissa is a condiment of North African provenance made with dried chiles, and usually remarkably spicy. Our recipe isn't too spicy, but it is authentically tasty. Try it with our Lamb Meatloaf (page 129), Zhug (page 105), and some Labne (page 76)—it makes a good sandwich, too.

When we made this, we strained the paste to keep it from being too watery. The harissa juice is a zingy flavoring for chili and soups like Vegetarian Matzo Ball. We have known cooks to drink it when feeling sniffly or use it to make kombucha.

Makes about 1 cup harissa and 1 to 1½ cups juice

2 fresh chiles, stemmed*

2 red bell peppers, stemmed and seeded

2 cloves garlic, peeled and minced

1 tablespoon Diamond Crystal kosher salt
    or 1½ teaspoons other kosher salt

1½ teaspoons ground cinnamon

1 teaspoon coriander seeds, or ¾ teaspoon ground coriander**

1 teaspoon caraway seeds, or ¾ teaspoon ground caraway**

1½ teaspoons olive oil

1½ teaspoons fresh lemon juice

We generally used poblanos or Anaheims. For a truer-to-form harissa, use jalapeños, serranos, or even dried guajillos (toasted in a dry skillet, soaked in hot water until soft, and drained before use). The heat is up to you; seed the chiles if you want less.

**Optional, but recommended: Dry-toast the coriander and caraway seeds in a skillet over medium heat until fragrant, a minute or so. (Please see page 105 for my feelings about spice toasting.) Grind in a spice grinder or blender when cool.*

Coarsely chop the chiles and bell peppers and place in a blender jar. Add the garlic, salt, cinnamon, coriander, and caraway. Add up to a ½ cup of water and blend to a uniform puree. Taste and add the olive oil and lemon juice to taste.

Line a strainer with cheesecloth and place it over a bowl. Pour in the puree and cover with plastic wrap. Refrigerate overnight to drain off the juice.

Store the harissa paste and juice in separate covered containers in the refrigerator for up to a week. Both can be frozen for up to a month without affecting quality.

Crème Fraîche

Real crème fraîche requires fresh cow's milk that is allowed to sour under controlled conditions. This is a mock crème fraîche recipe using pasteurized products. It couldn't be easier and works like a charm. This is a good thing to set up overnight.

Makes 1 cup

½ cup heavy cream
½ cup sour cream

Whisk the heavy cream and sour cream together thoroughly in a small bowl. Cover with plastic wrap or a clean flour sack towel. Let sit for 12 to 18 hours at room temperature, 72° to 78°F; this will allow the cultures in the sour cream to thicken and sour the heavy cream. Transfer to a covered container and refrigerate for up to a week.

Sweet Crème Fraîche

I use this in place of whipped cream, as I like the taste of sour, even in desserts. This is easiest in a stand mixer, but a hand mixer, old-fashioned egg beater, or a strong arm with a whisk work, too.

Makes about 2½ cups

1 cup heavy cream
⅓ cup powdered sugar
1 teaspoon vanilla extract
⅓ cup sour cream

Combine the heavy cream and sugar in the bowl of a stand mixer fitted with the whisk attachment. (Or in a mixing bowl if you're using a hand mixer, egg beater, or whisk.) Whip on medium-high speed until it's thick and makes soft peaks. Mix in the vanilla and sour cream. Use immediately, or cover and store in the refrigerator for up to a day (it may deflate slightly).

"Soft peaks" means peaks that don't remain standing when you lift the whisk, but softly curl over.

Mustard Crème Fraîche

First you need to make pickled mustard seeds, which are also featured in our Schmears (page 71) and are a piquant addition to sauces, vinaigrettes, and other dressings. This is a lovely sauce for a roast, but we most often garnished our Potato and Caramelized Onion Knishes with it.

Pickled Mustard Seeds

Makes about 1½ cups pickled mustard seeds

> ½ cup brown or yellow mustard seeds*
>
> ¼ cup vinegar**
>
> ½ cup granulated sugar

> *We found brown mustard seeds at the local international market or online. But it's okay to use yellow if you can't find brown.*
>
> **Any kind of vinegar works; we used apple cider most often because it is cheap and tasty.*

Toast the mustard seeds in a dry skillet over medium-high heat until they start popping a bit. Add the vinegar, sugar and ¾ cup water. Bring to a boil, stirring to dissolve the sugar. Remove from the heat and let cool. Store in a covered container in the refrigerator; these will last for months.

Mustard Crème Fraîche

Makes about 1½ cups crème fraîche

> 1 cup Crème Fraîche (page 112)
>
> 2 tablespoons Dijon mustard
>
> 1½ tablespoons drained Pickled Mustard Seeds (above) + 1 teaspoon brine

Whisk the crème fraîche, mustard, mustard seeds, and brine together in a small bowl. Cover and refrigerate. This keeps for at least a week.

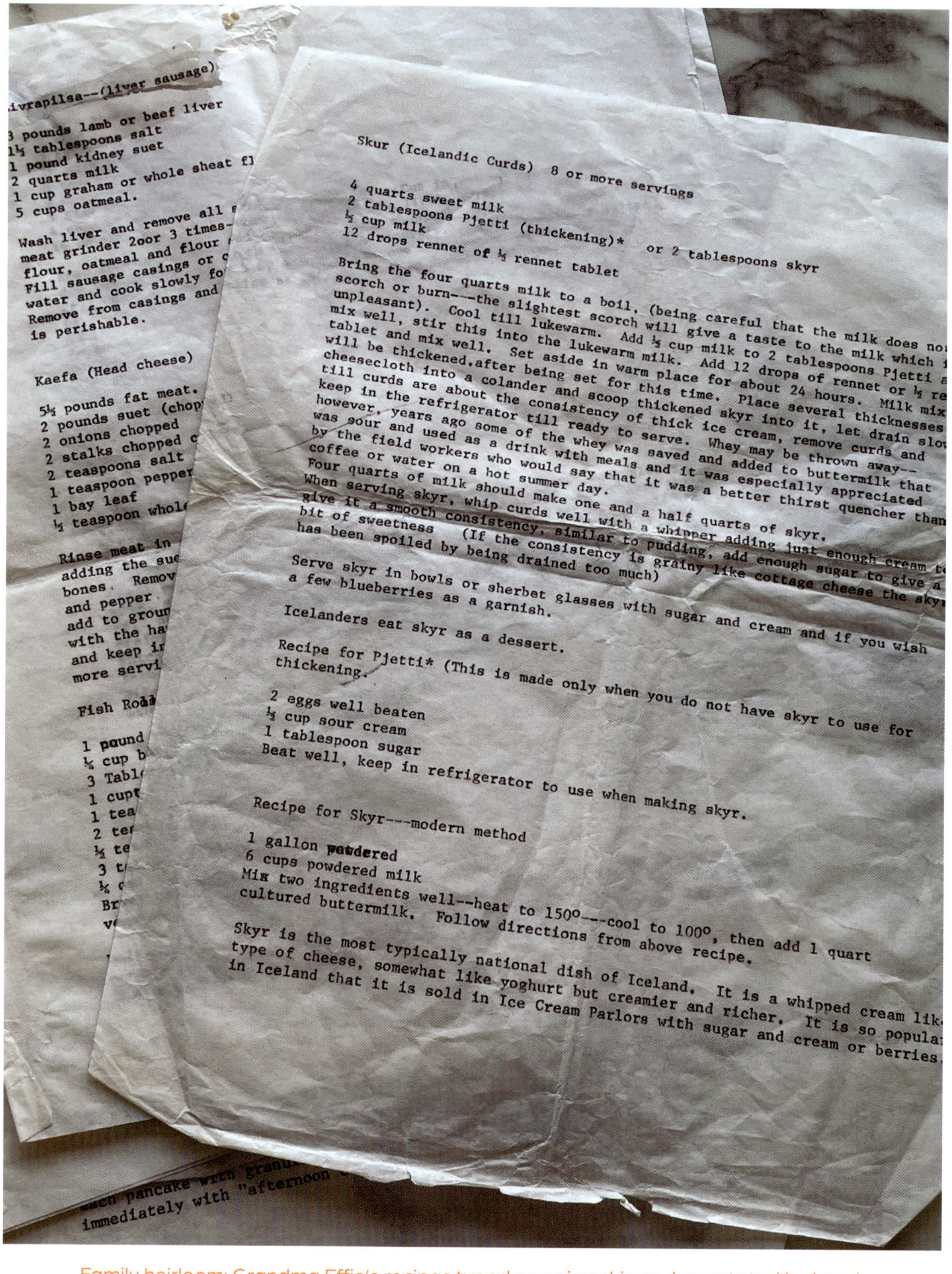

ivrapilsa--(liver sausage)

3 pounds lamb or beef liver
1½ tablespoons salt
1 pound kidney suet
2 quarts milk
1 cup graham or whole sheat fl
5 cups oatmeal.

Wash liver and remove all s
meat grinder 2oor 3 times-
flour, oatmeal and flour
Fill sausage casings or c
water and cook slowly fo
Remove from casings and
is perishable.

Kaefa (Head cheese)

5½ pounds fat meat.
2 pounds suet (chop
2 onions chopped
2 stalks chopped c
2 teaspoons salt
1 teaspoon pepper
1 bay leaf
½ teaspoon whole

Rinse meat in
adding the sue
bones. Remov
and pepper.
add to groun
with the ha
and keep in
more servi

Fish Roll

1 pound
¼ cup b
3 Table
1 cup
1 tea
2 te
½ te
3 t
¼ c
Br
ve

Skur (Icelandic Curds) 8 or more servings

4 quarts sweet milk
2 tablespoons Pjetti (thickening)*   or 2 tablespoons skyr
½ cup milk
12 drops rennet of ½ rennet tablet

Bring the four quarts milk to a boil, (being careful that the milk does not scorch or burn---the slightest scorch will give a taste to the milk which is unpleasant). Cool till lukewarm. Add ½ cup milk to 2 tablespoons Pjetti and mix well, stir this into the lukewarm milk. Add 12 drops of rennet or ½ rennet tablet and mix well. Set aside in warm place for about 24 hours. Milk mixture will be thickened, after being set for this time. Place several thicknesses of cheesecloth into a colander and scoop thickened skyr into it, let drain slowly till curds are about the consistency of thick ice cream, remove curds and keep in the refrigerator till ready to serve. Whey may be thrown away--however, years ago some of the whey was saved and added to buttermilk that was sour and used as a drink with meals and it was especially appreciated by the field workers who would say that it was a better thirst quencher than coffee or water on a hot summer day.
Four quarts of milk should make one and a half quarts of skyr.
When serving skyr, whip curds well with a whipper adding just enough cream to give it a smooth consistency, similar to pudding.   (If the consistency is grainy like cottage cheese the skyr bit of sweetness   has been spoiled by being drained too much) add enough sugar to give a
Serve skyr in bowls or sherbet glasses with sugar and cream and if you wish a few blueberries as a garnish.

Icelanders eat skyr as a dessert.

Recipe for Pjetti* (This is made only when you do not have skyr to use for thickening.

2 eggs well beaten
½ cup sour cream
1 tablespoon sugar
Beat well, keep in refrigerator to use when making skyr.

Recipe for Skyr---modern method

1 gallon powdered
6 cups powdered milk
Mix two ingredients well--heat to 150⁰---cool to 100⁰, then add 1 quart cultured buttermilk. Follow directions from above recipe.

Skyr is the most typically national dish of Iceland. It is a whipped cream like type of cheese, somewhat like yoghurt but creamier and richer. It is so popular in Iceland that it is sold in Ice Cream Parlors with sugar and cream or berries.

each pancake with grandm
immediately with "afternoon

Family heirloom: Grandma Effie's recipes typed on onion skin and annotated by hand.

Grandma Effie's Skyr

Skyr is an Icelandic fresh yogurt cheese (just like labne is in the Middle East) that you can find in your grocery store's yogurt aisle. Skyr is wonderful on its own, with granola, nuts, and berries for a snack, or as a slightly sour counterpoint for dishes like Swedish meatballs or smoked fish.

Save the whey; we sometimes added it to dressings. My grandma writes that it was added to buttermilk, and appreciated as a great thirst quencher on a hot summer day.

Makes 3 cups

> 2 quarts + ½ cup whole milk (preferably organic and
> not ultra-pasteurized)
>
> 1 tablespoon skyr*
>
> 6 drops liquid rennet or ¼ rennet tablet (optional)**

> *We used Siggi's, or 1 tablespoon reserved from a previous batch.*
> **Unless you have a cheesemaking store nearby, try Amazon. To make this
> without rennet, double the amount of skyr starter to 2 tablespoons.*

Bring 2 quarts of the milk to a simmer slowly over medium heat. (Be careful not to scorch or burn it, as the flavor will remain in the finished skyr.) Remove from the heat and cool to lukewarm, about 100°F.

Stir the skyr into the remaining ½ cup milk until blended. Add to the lukewarm milk along with the rennet and mix well. Cover with a clean flour sack towel and set aside at room temperature for 12 to 18 hours, until you can see that the skyr has separated into curds and whey.

To drain, use a fine-mesh chinois (conical strainer) or line a colander with a triple layer of cheesecloth. Place the chinois in its stand, or place the colander in the sink or over a deep bowl. Scoop in the thickened skyr and place in the refrigerator to let it drain overnight and no longer than three days. The curds should be about the consistency of thick sour cream.

Store the curds and whey in separate covered containers in the refrigerator for up to 1 week.

Sweet Skyr

Grandma Effie would whip drained curds with just enough heavy cream to make a very creamy pudding, and just enough sugar to give it a bit of sweetness. She recommends serving it in sherbet glasses, which I agree makes for the most charming old-school plating, but if you don't have these rarely useful pieces of glassware, just use a pretty bowl. This is my approximation of her haiku-like recipe.

Serves 4

> 2 cups Grandma Effie's Skyr (page 115)
>
> ⅓ cup heavy cream
>
> ¼ cup powdered sugar
>
> 2 cups assorted berries in season or any fruit you deem tasty,
>   or 1 cup lingonberry or currant preserves, for serving

With a whisk or a hand mixer on medium high speed, whisk the skyr, heavy cream, and sugar together until thick and creamy, 3 to 5 minutes by hand or 1 to 2 minutes with a mixer. Spoon into 4 individual small bowls or a serving bowl and top with berries or preserves. Serve immediately.

Grandma Effie in her office, 1977.

Apple–Ginger Compote

We served this alongside latkes, but you could use it with anything that requires a fruit sauce.

Makes about 2 cups

> 2 apples,* washed, halved, and cored
>
> ¾ teaspoon Diamond Crystal kosher salt
>   or ½ teaspoon other kosher salt
>
> 1 teaspoon canola oil
>
> 1 stalk rhubarb, leaves trimmed off, coarsely chopped (optional)**
>
> 2 teaspoons minced candied ginger (aka crystallized ginger)
>
> ¼ cup granulated sugar
>
> *We used Honeycrisp or Gala apples because I like a crisp and tart apple.
>
> **We added rhubarb when there was way too much in the summer. It will make the compote tarter.

Cut apples into thin wedges, at least 8 per half apple. Place in a bowl and toss with the salt. Let sit for 15 to 20 minutes, until they have sweat a bit.

Heat a wide-bottomed saucepan over medium heat. Add the oil and swirl to coat the bottom of the pan. Add the apples, the rhubarb (if using), and the ginger. Stir with a wooden spoon while lightly frying the apples. After about 3 minutes, add the sugar and stir to combine well. Reduce the heat and cook until the apples look slightly candied and sort of translucent, but not mushy, about 10 to 15 minutes more. Remove from the heat and let cool to room temperature.

Store in a covered container in the refrigerator for up to a week.

Sandwiches

As a sincere sandwich lover, I have my own ideas about what to put between two slices of bread: not too much meat or cheese (no Dagwoods!), a zippy condiment or two—and pickles are necessary. It is important to limit the number of soggy things like tomato slices or pickled onions, and to make sure that they are nestled where they won't make the bread fall apart. For example, we put the sauerkraut on our Brisket Sandwich between the meat and cheese so that it was safe from sopping the bread. We also used a hearty rye bread, which could probably stand up to some wet sauerkraut anyhow.

Egg Salad

We served our version open-faced, topped with capers, shaved onion, cucumber, and microgreens.

Makes 2 cups, enough for 4 sandwiches

> 1½ teaspoons Diamond Crystal kosher salt
>   or 1¼ teaspoons other kosher salt
> 7 large eggs
> ¼ cup minced celery (1 stalk)
> ¼ cup minced fennel tops with fronds (2 fennel fronds)
> ¼ cup minced scallions, green and white parts both (3 scallions)
> 1½ tablespoons Dijon mustard
> 3 tablespoons mayonnaise
> 2 turns of a pepper mill

Fill a bowl two-thirds full of ice and water. (You'll need this ice water bath to quick-chill the cooked eggs.)

Fill a large saucepan with water to a depth of 2 inches and add 1 teaspoon of the salt. Bring to a boil over high heat. Carefully add the eggs, cover the pan, and reduce heat to maintain a simmer. Simmer the eggs for 11 to 12 minutes. Remove from the heat and drain the eggs in a colander, then place them in the ice water bath until cool.

Peel the eggs. Place them in a large bowl and chop them with a pastry blender into ¼-inch to ½-inch pieces. (If you don't have a pastry blender, chop them with a knife on a cutting board, then transfer them to a large bowl.)

I find it easier to peel eggs with my hands under running water.

Add the celery, fennel, scallions, mustard, 2 tablespoons of the mayo, the remaining salt, and the pepper. Mix well; add an additional tablespoon of mayo if it seems too dry. (The texture you want depends on the heartiness of the bread. If you are serving this on a bagel, you will want a firmer filling so that it doesn't squish out of the sides.)

Store in a closed container in the refrigerator for up to 4 days.

Smoked Trout Salad

This is BernBaum's version of smoked whitefish salad, a favorite of our downtown business neighbor and friend Greg Danz. We used trout, as it is locally plentiful and easier to debone than whitefish. However, this recipe also works with smoked whitefish and Hot-Smoked Salmon. We topped this with Pickled Apples, cucumber, and microgreens for a sandwich.

Like most fish salads, this is great as a melt: Place ¼ cup of the salad on each piece of bread, top with cheese, and broil until the cheese is melted. It's also great for a nosh on some bagel chips. Add smoked salmon and some capers and you have a nice little fish plate.

Before you start working with the trout, glove your hands unless you want to smell smoked fish on everything you touch for the next 24 hours.

Makes about 2 cups, enough for 4 generous sandwiches

>¾ pound smoked trout fillet (with skin and bones)
>
>1 stalk celery, cut on the bias ⅛ inch thick (¼ cup)
>
>1 stalk fennel with fronds (not the bulb), sliced ⅛ inch thick (¼ cup)
>
>1 small shallot, peeled and minced (2 tablespoons)
>
>2 tablespoons chopped fresh dill
>
>1½ scallions (green and white parts), sliced ⅛ inch thick
>
>Grated zest and juice of 1 to 2 lemons
>
>2 tablespoons sour cream
>
>2 tablespoons mayonnaise
>
>4 turns of a pepper mill
>
>½ teaspoon Diamond Crystal kosher salt
> or ¼ teaspoon other kosher salt

**Smoked fish is usually salty enough and doesn't need additional salt.*

recipe continues

Greg Danz, friend and longtime proprietor of Zandbroz Variety,
the best thing to happen in the old Leeby's building since Leeby's.

Pull off and discard the skin from the trout fillet. Gently pull out the spine and its attached feathery bones. Depending on the size of the fillet, there may be another line of pin bones running along the length of the fillet, starting at the head end and ending about two-thirds of the way down. Pull these out gently with your fingers or tweezers. Break the fillet into a large bowl; you should have about 2 cups flaked fish.

> *I usually touch the thickest part of the fillet with my finger to see if I can feel the pin bones, and pull out what I can. Then I break off pieces of flesh and place them in a bowl, looking and feeling for pin bones as I go along. I go through the deboned fish at least two times to ensure that I have pulled out all of the bones.*

Add the celery, fennel fronds, shallot, dill, scallions, and lemon zest and juice to the trout and mix gently. Add the sour cream and 1 tablespoon of the mayo and mix well. (The salad should be evenly moistened but not so wet that it will squish out of the bagel when made into a sandwich.) Add the rest of the mayo if the salad is dry. Season with the pepper and a touch of salt, if you think it needs it.

Store in a covered container in the refrigerator for up to 4 days.

Chicken Walnut Salad

This is my attempt to make a deli salad out of a Turkish recipe for Circassian chicken that I learned from a family friend, Sara Hanhan. It's simpler than the original, but has tremendous flavor from the combination of ground walnuts and spices. Sara is a friend of my mother's from grade school—a friendship of seventy years—who went into the Peace Corps in Turkey, where she met her husband, Uğur. They returned to North Dakota when their children were young, bringing the beauty of Turkish food and culture to a place that needed it.

This is a great side for a green salad, and is a wonderful sandwich melt; use ¼ cup of salad per piece of bread, cover with the cheese of your choice, and broil until melted and golden. We served ours with Pickled Apple slices, cucumber, and microgreens.

Sara and Uğur Hanhan in Istanbul, March 1972. Uğur's mom is giving their three–month–old son Kenan a bottle.

Makes about 2 cups, enough for 4 sandwiches

> ¾ cup toasted walnuts
>
> 1 clove garlic, peeled and minced
>
> 1½ teaspoons smoked paprika
>
> 1½ teaspoons paprika
>
> ¾ teaspoon ground cumin (toasted if you like; see page 105)
>
> 1¼ cups chopped poached chicken, in ½-inch pieces (8 ounces)*
>
> ½ shallot, peeled and minced
>
> 3 tablespoons minced fennel or fennel fronds
>
> 1 stalk celery, minced (¼ cup)
>
> 2 scallions, both green and white parts, sliced thinly
>
> ⅓ cup mayonnaise
>
> 3 tablespoons plain yogurt
>
> 1 teaspoon fresh lemon juice, plus more if needed
>
> ½ to 1 teaspoon Diamond Crystal kosher salt
>   or ¼ to ½ teaspoon other kosher salt
>
> 2 or 3 turns of a pepper mill

> *If you poach a whole chicken for Myron's Chicken Matzo Ball Soup (page 175), you will have at least a half pound left for this recipe. You can also use rotisserie chicken from the local deli. Remove all the skin, bones, and cartilage before chopping the chicken.*

Add the walnuts, garlic, smoked paprika, paprika, and cumin to the work bowl of a food processor. Pulse until the walnuts are ground into coarse meal.

Place the chicken in a large bowl. Add the walnut mixture and mix well with your gloved hands or a spatula. Add the shallots, fennel, celery, scallions, mayo, yogurt, and lemon juice. Mix until all the ingredients are well combined. Season to taste with salt, pepper and possibly a bit more lemon.

Store in a covered container in the refrigerator for up to 4 days.

Lamb Meatloaf

This Nordic–inspired dish is the gateway for many skeptical lamb eaters, probably because it's usually served with jam and pickled onions. This is a basic meatloaf recipe, which makes it perfect to gussy up, either as slices of meatloaf (with or without gravy) to serve as an entree plate or as a sandwich filling, or as meatballs with gravy. Serve the meatloaf with lingonberry sauce or Zhug (page 105), roasted potatoes, and pickles; serve the meatballs with mashed potatoes, lingonberry sauce, and a relish plate.

Makes one 8½ × 4½-inch loaf, enough for 4 to 6 sandwiches;
or 30 small (1-ounce) meatballs or 15 larger (2-ounce) meatballs, to serve 4 to 6

Lamb Meatloaf or Meatballs

⅓ cup heavy cream

2 large eggs

4 teaspoons honey

⅔ cup homemade breadcrumbs*

1 tablespoon Diamond Crystal kosher salt
    or 1½ teaspoons other kosher salt

4 turns of a pepper mill

1 tablespoon canola oil

1 small onion, diced small (about ⅔ cup)

⅓ cup small-diced fennel bulb, stalk, and fronds

4 teaspoons minced fresh dill or ½ teaspoon dried dill weed

1½ pounds ground lamb**

12 ounces ground pork

Nonstick cooking spray, additional canola oil, or unsalted butter

Sour Cream Gravy, for serving (optional; recipe follows)

*We made ours out of day-old focaccia, blitzed in a food processor,
    but Japanese-style panko breadcrumbs will work, too.
**You can use beef or bison instead.

recipe continues

Whisk the cream, eggs, and honey together in a medium bowl. Add the breadcrumbs, salt, and pepper, and stir to combine. Cover and refrigerate for at least an hour or up to a day; this is the panade (a starch and liquid mixture that will lighten and bind the meat mixture).

While the panade rests, heat a skillet over medium-high heat. Add the oil, onion, fennel, and dill, and cook for 5 to 8 minutes, until tender but without coloring. Remove from heat to cool.

Combine the panade, onion mixture, lamb, and pork in a large bowl or the bowl of a stand mixer. If mixing by hand, use your gloved hands to mix until uniform. If using a mixer, attach the paddle and mix on low to medium speed until well combined. It is important to knead in the panade so that there aren't bread chunks in the finished loaf.

MAKING AS A MEATLOAF: Preheat the oven to 350°. Spray or oil an 8½ × 4½-inch loaf pan. Scoop the meat mixture the loaf pan and press on it to form an evenly dense loaf. Place the pan on a baking sheet (to keep the oven clean). Place this in the middle rack of the oven and bake until the center of the loaf has reached 140°, 20 to 25 minutes (check with an instant-read thermometer). Remove from the oven. To serve the meatloaf now, carefully remove it from the pan with a large, wide spatula; if you like, use the juices in the pan to make the gravy. (See the headnote for serving suggestions.)

To reserve for later use or for sandwiches, let the meatloaf cool in the pan for about 30 minutes at room temperature. Take it out of the loaf pan and place on a clean plate or dish. If you like, refrigerate the juices from the pan in a closed container before using them to make the gravy. Refrigerate the meatloaf until completely cooled. You can then double-wrap it in plastic and freeze for up to 1 month, or keep it refrigerated for up to 4 days. Defrost in the refrigerator before slicing to serve or use in sandwiches.

MAKING AS MEATBALLS: Use a 1- or 2-ounce scoop or a large soup spoon to scoop out 30 small or 15 larger portions. Roll the portions in your gloved hands to round the meatballs. Place on a baking sheet and refrigerate until you're ready to cook.

To bake the meatballs, preheat the oven to 350°F. Place the baking sheet on the middle rack and bake for 10 to 12 minutes, until browned on the surface and cooked to the center (just the barest hint of pink). If you like, use the browned bits from the pan to make the gravy. Serve immediately with or without the gravy. Or let cool to room temperature and store in a covered container in the refrigerator for up to a few days, or freeze for up to a month.

To cook them on the stovetop, heat a wide sauté pan over medium-high heat. Add a swirl of canola oil or butter and heat until the oil is shimmering or the butter is foaming. Working in batches, drop the meatballs into the pan, leaving an inch of space around each meatball so that they can brown evenly. Turn the meatballs to brown all sides, about 4 to 7 minutes. Remove each batch and set it aside on a clean baking sheet, then brown another batch until all the meatballs have been browned. If serving in gravy, set aside the pan with the browned bits to make the gravy, then finish cooking the meatballs in the gravy, 3 to 5 minutes until fully cooked. If serving immediately without gravy, return all the meatballs to the pan, reduce the heat to medium low, cover, and cook the meatballs completely, an additional 3 to 5 minutes.

You can reserve the meatballs in a closed container in the refrigerator or freezer to serve at a later time. They last a few days in the refrigerator or up to a month in the freezer.

Fellow doctors and longtime colleagues Thom Marubbio (left) and Dad at BernBaum's.
Thom grew up in Brooklyn, so he knows from a bagel.

Sour Cream Gravy

I like to make this Scandinavian complement to meatballs in the same sauté pan in which I browned the meatballs.

Makes about 2 cups, enough for 4 servings

> 3 cups homemade (page 176) or store-bought chicken stock*
>
> 2 tablespoons unsalted butter
>
> Browned bits from the meatloaf or meatball pan (if possible)
>
> 1 batch Lamb Meatloaf or Meatballs (page 129)
>
> ¼ cup Crème Fraîche (page 112) or sour cream
>
> 1 tablespoon chopped fresh herbs (like parsley, dill, fennel fronds, chives, and/or tarragon)
>
> **If using bouillon cubes and water or salted store-bought stock, use 1½ cups and do not reduce it, as it will get too salty. Just bring it up to a simmer before adding it to the meatballs.*

Bring the stock to a simmer in a small saucepan over medium-high heat. Reduce the heat to maintain a simmer until the stock has reduced by half. (You need about 1½ cups for the gravy.)

When you're ready to serve, heat the pan you used to brown the meatballs or a clean, wide sauté pan over medium-high heat. Add the butter; once it is foaming, add the meatballs if you're serving them. (If you baked the meatloaf or meatballs, add the reserved juices from that pan.) Add the reduced stock and simmer until the gravy looks slightly reduced and thicker. Swirl in the crème fraîche and herbs and remove from the heat. Stir until the gravy is completely emulsified. Serve immediately with the meatballs or over sliced meatloaf.

Nordic Lamb Sandwich

1 batch Lamb Meatloaf (page 129), cooked and chilled

Canola oil, for frying (optional)

4 pieces Focaccia (page 26), split

½ to ¾ cup mayonnaise

½ to ¾ cup lingonberry preserves

1 cup drained Red Onion pickles (page 78)

Other Sweet Brine Pickles of your choice (page 78), for serving

Preheat the oven to 400°F.

Slice the meatloaf to about ½- to ¾-inch thickness. Place them in one layer on a baking sheet. Bake for 4 to 6 minutes, until heated throughout. (You can also pan-fry them in a little oil, in batches, to heat and brown them, turning them once.)

At the same time, place the focaccia cut side up on a baking sheet. Toast in the oven for 4 to 6 minutes, until warm and toasted on the edges. Remove from the oven and place on individual plates.

Spread mayonnaise on the cut side of the focaccia bottoms and lingonberries on the tops. Place 2 slices of meatloaf on top of the mayonnaise and add a generous amount of pickled onions. Top with the top part of the focaccia, slice in half, and serve with sweet pickles.

Israeli Lamb Sandwich

This Israeli counterpoint to our Nordic Lamb Sandwich deploys a mash-up of our house-made condiments and was a staff favorite.

Makes 4 sandwiches

> 1 batch Lamb Meatloaf (page 129), cooked and chilled
>
> Canola oil, for frying (optional)
>
> 4 pieces Focaccia (page 26), split
>
> ¾ to 1 cup Labne (page 76), or store-bought
>
> ½ to ¾ cup Fresh Pepper Harissa (page 110), or store-bought
>
> 12 thin slices seedless cucumber
>
> ½ cup Zhug (page 105)
>
> 2 cups salad greens, washed and spun dry
>
> Generous pinch of kosher salt (any brand)
>
> 2 tablespoons Ladolemono (page 225)
>
> Pickles of your choice (pages 77 to 82), for serving

Preheat the oven to 400°F.

Slice the meatloaf so that you get around 8 slices of ½- to ¾-inch thickness. Place them in one layer on a baking sheet. Bake for 4 to 6 minutes, until heated throughout. (You can also pan-fry them in a little oil, in batches, to heat and brown them, turning them once.)

At the same time, place focaccia cut side up on a baking sheet. Toast in the oven for 4 to 6 minutes, until warm and toasted on the edges. Remove from the oven and place on individual plates.

Spread labne on the cut side of the focaccia bottoms and harissa on the tops. Place 3 cucumber slices atop the labne, and 2 meatloaf slices atop the cucumber. Spoon a bit of zhug on top of the meatloaf and top with the top part of the focaccia. Slice in half and place on individual plates.

Toss the greens with salt and ladolemono. Serve a handful of greens between the two halves of each sandwich, with pickles on the side.

Chicken Schnitzel Sandwich

Who doesn't like fried chicken? We used matzo meal to give a crisp coating to thin pieces of chicken breast and we served the schnitzel as an entree with Horseradish–Caraway Potato Salad, lingonberry preserves, Kraut Tzatziki, and a sweet cucumber pickle. For the sandwich, we toasted a challah bun, slathered it with mayo, Kraut Tzatziki, and lingonberry preserves, and served it with the same sides.

Makes 4 schnitzels, for 4 sandwiches

Chicken Schnitzel

½ cup all-purpose flour

1 tablespoon + 2 teaspoons Diamond Crystal kosher salt
    or 2½ teaspoons other kosher salt, plus more for sprinkling

⅛ teaspoon freshly ground black pepper

3 large eggs

1½ cups matzo meal

1 teaspoon Hawaij Spice Mix (page 92)

2 boneless, skinless chicken breasts (5 to 6 ounces each),
    split into cutlets and pounded

3 to 4 cups canola or other vegetable oil, for frying

To split a chicken breast into cutlets, lay it flat on a cutting board. Put the hand not holding the knife on top, palm down, fingers flexed upward, to hold it in place. Carefully slice through the chicken breast horizontally (parallel to the cutting board) so that you get two roughly equal cutlets, each half as thick as the original breast. (Sometimes the breasts are giant enough that you can get three cutlets out of one breast.)

To pound, one at a time, place a cutlet on a cutting board, cover with plastic wrap, and pound with a mallet or small frypan to an even ¼-inch thickness.

Whisk the flour, 2 teaspoons of the Diamond Crystal or 1 teaspoon other salt, and the pepper together in a pie plate, loaf pan, or rimmed dish. Beat the eggs in another container like the first until well blended. Combine the matzo meal, the remaining salt, and the hawaij in a third container. (This is your breading station.) Line a baking sheet with parchment paper.

recipe continues

Working with one chicken cutlet at a time, dip both sides in the seasoned flour to coat, shake off any excess, then place the cutlet in the eggs. Use tongs to flip the cutlet and make sure that both sides are coated with egg, then pull it out and let excess egg drip off. Coat both sides with matzo meal, shake off any excess, and place on the prepared baking sheet. Repeat with the remaining chicken. Once all the schnitzels are breaded, you can refrigerate them for up to 8 hours before frying, covered with plastic wrap.

When you're ready to fry, line a platter or another baking sheet with several layers of paper towels. Pour oil to a depth of about ½ inch into a large cast-iron skillet or other heavy, wide-bottomed pan. Heat the oil over medium-high heat to 325°F. To test if it is frying temperature, drop a crouton-size bit of bread into the oil. If it sizzles and turns golden immediately, the oil is ready.

Add the schnitzels one at a time, shaking the pan gently to allow the oil to shimmer over the top. (If you won't be able to fit all four schnitzels in a single layer, fry them in batches.) Fry on both sides, turning once with tongs, to a light golden color (about 4 minutes total) before transferring them to the paper towels to drain. Cut into one to check that it is opaque white inside and cooked throughout; if not, return the schnitzel to the oil for 1 to 2 minutes until fully cooked. Sprinkle with salt before serving. If you won't be serving the schnitzels immediately, let them cool, then transfer to a baking sheet. You can cover them with plastic wrap and refrigerate for up to 4 days. They can be stored in a resealable plastic bag and frozen for up to a month. Defrost in the refrigerator.

Sandwich

4 Chicken Schnitzels (above)

4 Challah Rolls (page 29), split

½ to ¾ cup mayonnaise

½ to ¾ cup Kraut Tzatziki (page 91)

Kosher salt (any brand)

½ to ¾ cup lingonberry preserves

1 cup drained Bread and Butter Pickles (page 82)

2 cups Horseradish-Caraway Potato Salad (page 232)

Preheat the oven to 400°F. If the schnitzels have cooled or been refrigerated, place them on a baking sheet to rewarm in the oven. Place the challah rolls cut side up on a baking sheet. Put both in the oven for 3 to 5 minutes, until the schnitzels are warmed through and the rolls are lightly toasted. Remove both from the oven.

Spread mayo on the roll bottoms and tzatziki on the tops. Sprinkle the chicken pieces with salt and place on the bottoms. Close the sandwiches, cut in half, and place each on a plate. Serve with the lingonberry preserves, pickles, and a scoop of potato salad on the side.

Turkey Pastrami Sandwich

Traditionally, pastrami is smoked. However, this recipe works without smoking and still delivers a great sandwich filling—I guess you could call it corned turkey. Brining is a method of delivering salt and flavor throughout the meat. In this case, it ensures a moist and flavorful turkey breast with a spicy pepper crust. You could substitute a whole 2½-pound chicken or a 2-pound piece of brisket, with or without smoking. For chicken, brine for only a day or two at most. This recipe takes a minimum of 3 days.

Makes about 1 pound pastrami, enough for 4 generous sandwiches (and then some)

Turkey Pastrami

3 tablespoons Diamond Crystal kosher salt
  or 4½ teaspoons other kosher salt

3 tablespoons granulated sugar

1½ packed tablespoons brown sugar

½ teaspoon pickling spice

2 teaspoons honey

1 clove garlic, unpeeled, smashed with the side of a knife blade

1 to 1½ pounds boneless, skinless turkey breast, in one piece*

2 teaspoons coriander seeds, lightly toasted (see page 105)

2 teaspoons black peppercorns, lightly toasted (see page 105)

Nonstick cooking spray (optional)

Try to find one that isn't pumped up with water, salt, and other additives.

Combine the salt, granulated and brown sugars, pickling spice, honey, and garlic with 3 cups water in a medium saucepan. Bring to a simmer, stirring to dissolve salt and sugars. Remove from heat and allow to cool to room temperature, then refrigerate until chilled.

Use a container large enough to fit the turkey breast snugly but with space for the brine. Place the turkey breast in the container and pour the brine over it. Cover with a layer of plastic wrap directly on the turkey and top with a few plates or something heavy enough to keep it below the surface of the brine. Refrigerate for at least 2 days but no more than 3 days.

Transfer the turkey to a paper towel–lined baking sheet or plate. Discard the brine. Pat the turkey dry on all sides. Refrigerate for a day uncovered so that the outside will dry and allow the spices and smoke to adhere to it during cooking.

Combine the coriander and black pepper in a spice grinder or high-powered blender and pulse until coarsely ground. Rub this all over the turkey breast, covering all sides.

Smoking the turkey (optional): Preheat your smoker, following the manufacturer's directions. Meanwhile, soak 2 cups wood chips, chunks, or pellets in water for at least 15 minutes, then drain well. (If you're using a stovetop smoker, use about 2 tablespoons unsoaked wood chips.) Add the wood to the smoker according to directions. Place the grate at least 8 inches above the heat source and spray it with nonstick cooking spray. Place the turkey breast atop and close the cover. It should take 30 to 45 minutes to fully cook and smoke turkey, at a temperature of around 300 °F. You want to get as heavy a smoke flavor as possible, so replace the chips as needed. (Using the Big Green Egg at home, I do this by adding new chips every 30 minutes.)

recipe continues

Smoke the turkey to an internal temperature of 150°F. Remove from the smoker, place on a platter, and let cool to room temperature.

Roasting the turkey (optional, if not smoking): Preheat the oven to 350°F. Place the turkey on a roasting rack in a roasting pan and cook to an internal temperature of 150°F, 15 to 20 minutes. Remove from the oven and place on a platter. (The turkey will cook the remaining 15° to a safe 165°F, thanks to carryover cooking.) Let cool to room temperature.

If not using for sandwiches immediately, cover with plastic wrap and refrigerate for up to 5 days or freeze for up to a month.

Sandwich

12 ounces Turkey Pastrami (above)

1 cup Krautsalat (page 93)

8 slices brick or Swiss cheese

4 Challah Rolls (page 29), split

½ cup Russian Dressing (page 225)

Dill Brine Pickles (page 80), for serving

If the pastrami was frozen, defrost it overnight in the fridge.

Preheat the oven to broil. Line a baking sheet with foil.

Slice the pastrami as thin as you can. Place the slices in four equal piles on the prepared baking sheet and top with up to ¼ cup krautsalat. Place a slice or two of cheese atop the krautsalat. Place the challah rolls cut side up on a second baking sheet. Put the baking sheet with the turkey on an upper rack in the oven and the challah baking sheet below it. Broil until the cheese is melted (2 to 3 minutes in most ovens) and the rolls are toasted. (Watch them, as they may cook at different rates!)

Remove each baking sheet from the oven when done. Slather both cut sides of each roll with Russian dressing. Place a turkey-and-cheese bundle atop each bun bottom and cover with the bun top. Cut in half and serve with lots of dill pickles.

Breakfast All Day

We started with bagels at BernBaum's but gradually expanded our breakfast offerings to include things like eggs, latkes, and sweet–ish pastries for those who aren't bagel inclined. Weekend brunch became our bread and butter, when customers suffered the longer lines to get a table. Although I don't usually partake in breakfast (other than copious amounts of coffee and toast), I have always loved the sight of people getting together over a table laden with egg bake and breakfast sandwiches and, of course, lots of good coffee.

RAGE

Lox Scrambled Eggs

This is a lighter play on Jewish deli salami and eggs. I like cream in the scramble, but if you want a dairy-free version, add a splash of acid (in the form of sherry vinegar or lemon juice) to the eggs right before cooking to make them fluffier, and cook them in oil.

We added a few slices of cold-smoked cured salmon (otherwise known as Nova lox), capers, shaved onion, and microgreens to complete the plate. And, of course, a freshly baked bagel.

Serves 3 or 4

9 large eggs

¾ cup heavy cream

½ teaspoon Diamond Crystal kosher salt
or ¼ teaspoon other kosher salt

2 tablespoons butter

¾ cup flaked skinless hot-smoked salmon
(about 4 ounces)

1 tablespoon minced fresh tender herbs,
(parsley, scallion, dill, chervil,
or fennel fronds)

Pinch of flaky sea salt (such as Maldon)

Hot-smoked salmon is salmon that is cured, then cooked while it smokes, so its texture is firmer and it flakes easily. Cold-smoked salmon is cured and smoked at a low temperature so it resembles uncooked salmon; it is generally sold sliced, as lox. To make this more confusing, traditional lox is cured but not smoked. Nova lox, which we used, is cured and cold-smoked.

Break the eggs into a bowl and add the cream and kosher salt. Whisk well.

Heat a well-seasoned cast-iron or nonstick skillet over medium heat. Add the butter. Once it is foaming, reduce the heat to low and add the salmon, herbs, and flaky salt. When the salmon looks a little fried around the edges, add the egg mixture, making sure that the pan isn't too hot—you don't want the eggs to brown. Use a spatula to stir the eggs around the pan, scraping the bottom as you stir. The faster you stir, the smaller the curds will be. Remove from the heat while the eggs are still a little wet. Scrape onto plates or a serving dish and serve immediately.

Egg Bake

I originally thought our take on the Midwestern egg bake—a breakfast casserole—would house all of the day-old bagels like a savory bread pudding, but the dish turned out to be better without the bread. We changed it up depending on what we had around—any assortment of vegetables (roasted or sautéed), cheese, and maybe a bit of meat. We liked to serve it with Zhug and lemony greens.

With its fifty–fifty ratio of eggs to cream, this is like a custardy, crustless quiche.

Serves 4 to 6

6 large eggs

1½ cups heavy cream

1 teaspoon Diamond Crystal kosher salt or ¾ teaspoon other kosher salt

Unsalted butter or nonstick cooking spray, for the pan

1½ to 2 cups coarsely chopped roasted or sautéed vegetables*

1 cup grated cheese**

2 tablespoons chopped fresh herbs (parsley, chives, fennel fronds, or your favorite)

*If you like, replace some of the vegetables with chopped cooked meat.
**This is a great way to use up little bits of many cheeses.

Break the eggs into a bowl and whisk vigorously to break up the yolks. Add the cream and salt and whisk again until uniformly mixed. (A stick blender will make quick work of this.)

Preheat the oven to 350°F. Butter or spray a 10-inch quiche pan or pie plate. (You can also use a 9 × 9-inch baking pan.) Pour the egg mixture into the pan. Sprinkle the vegetables, then the cheese, evenly throughout the pan. Top with a scattering of fresh herbs and cover with foil.

Place on the middle rack of the oven and bake for 40 to 50 minutes, until barely set in the center of the pan. Remove from the oven and let it rest for 10 minutes before cutting into individual pieces if you are serving immediately.

You can bake this ahead, cool it completely, cover with plastic wrap, and refrigerate. To reheat, cover with foil, place in a 350°F oven, and bake for about 20 minutes, until hot. Alternatively, heat individual portions in the microwave on high for about 2 to 3 minutes.

Shakshuka Focaccia

A North African dish that is beloved in Israel, we made ours by poaching the egg in tomato sauce and then placing on a focaccia bun—a self-contained breakfast that happens to be vegetarian and dairy-free.

Serves 4 to 6, with 2 cups extra sauce for another use

Shakshuka Sauce

The tomato and pepper sauce is really versatile—it would be good on meatballs and pasta, a chicken breast, or any recipe where you would use tomato sauce.

¼ cup olive oil

1 small yellow onion, peeled and diced small

2 poblano peppers, stemmed, seeded, and diced small

4 cloves garlic, peeled and minced

1 tablespoon cumin, toasted and ground

1½ teaspoons smoked paprika

1 teaspoon urfa biber flakes

4 cups canned whole tomatoes with their juice,
    coarsely chopped or pureed

4 teaspoons Diamond Crystal kosher salt
    or 2 teaspoons other kosher salt

½ teaspoon freshly ground black pepper

Heat the olive oil in a large skillet over medium-low heat. Add onions and poblanos. Cook gently until very soft, about 15 minutes. Add the garlic and cook for an additional minute or two. Stir in cumin, paprika, and urfa biber. After a few minutes, pour in tomatoes and simmer until the sauce has thickened, about 10 minutes. Season with the salt and pepper. Remove from heat and allow to cool. If not using immediately, store in a closed container in the refrigerator for up to 4 days.

Focaccia and Eggs

Neutral oil (such as canola or olive), for the baking sheet

1 batch Focaccia dough (page 26), prepared through the first rise

¼ cup olive oil

½ batch Shakshuka Sauce (page 149)

4 to 6 large eggs (at least 1 per person or focaccia piece)

1 to 2 tablespoons za'atar

2 to 3 teaspoons flaky sea salt (such as Maldon)

2 cups salad greens, washed and spun dry

Pinch of kosher salt (any brand)

2 tablespoons Ladolemono (page 225)

Preheat the oven to 425°F. Generously oil a baking sheet.

Portion the focaccia dough into 4 to 6 clementine-size balls (roughly 5 ounces each) and place them on the baking sheet, spaced out from one another. Turn each ball over and use a ladle to create a center crater. Add a ladle or large spoonful or two of sauce, about 2 ounces per bun.

Bake the buns for about 12 minutes on the middle rack of the oven, rotating the baking sheet after about 6 minutes to ensure even baking, until fully baked and golden. Remove from the oven. Push down the center of each bun again with a spoon or ladle to recreate space for the eggs. Let cool.

Heat the shakshuka sauce in a wide saucepan or sauté pan over medium-high heat. (You may want to add up to ½ cup water if it seems too thick.) Once it is simmering, crack each of the eggs into a different quadrant (or sixth) of the saucepan. Reduce the heat to low, cover, and simmer for 4 to 5 minutes, until the eggs are poached to your preferred degree of doneness. (I cook them until the white is almost fully set but the yolk is still completely runny.)

Take the pan off the heat and spoon each of the eggs into a waiting focaccia bun. Top with a bit more sauce and sprinkles of za'atar and flaky salt. Toss the greens with the kosher salt and ladolemono. Place a loose handful of each on each plate.

Grandma Bonnie's Latkes

The highlight of Hanukkah—and maybe December—is Brett's mom's latkes. Bonnie grinds the potatoes instead of grating them, giving the latkes a substantial but soft filling inside of the crispy, fried crust. Our son measures all latkes against Grandma Bonnie's. Her batch feeds a family gathering of over twenty, so we have cut it down. (Every Hanukkah, Bonnie gives us foil-wrapped packages of latkes that we reheat at home.)

The latkes can be served with Crème Fraîche (page 112) and Apple–Ginger Compote (page 118), or sour cream and applesauce if that is easier. They are great with lox, capers, onions, and crème fraîche as well.

Latkes are not difficult to make, but it is important to work quickly as the potatoes will oxidize and turn pinkish red and then black, which makes for ugly latkes. I usually mix the eggs, salt, pepper, and baking powder together in a bowl before grinding or grating the potatoes. My sister grates her potatoes and onions into ice water, which keeps them from oxidizing until she's ready to mix the batter.

Makes 6 4-inch diameter latkes, and is easily doubled or tripled for a latke party

> 2 large eggs
>
> 1 tablespoon Diamond Crystal kosher salt
> or 1½ teaspoons other kosher salt
>
> ¼ teaspoon freshly ground black pepper
>
> ½ teaspoon baking powder
>
> 4 large floury potatoes (like russets; about 8 ounces each), peeled
>
> 1 small sweet yellow onion (about 5 ounces), peeled, halved,
> and root end trimmed
>
> Canola oil, for frying
>
> ¼ to ⅓ cup all-purpose flour

Preheat the oven to 325°F.

Combine the eggs, 2 teaspoons Diamond Crystal salt or 1 teaspoon other kosher salt, the pepper, and the baking powder in a small bowl. Whisk until well blended.

Grind the potatoes and onion together into another large bowl, or grate them on the large holes on a box grater. (You can also grate them in a food processor with the large grating disk and transfer them to a large bowl.) Add the remaining salt and mix well.

Let the potato-onion mixture sit to absorb salt and lose water for no more than
3 minutes while you set up your potato-wringing contraption: Center a clean flour
sack towel in a colander set inside another large bowl. Place a handful of the potato-
onion mixture (no more than 2 cups) in the towel. Gather the edges of the towel
together and twist to wring the liquid out of the mixture. Unwrap and add the drained
mixture to the eggs. Repeat until you have wrung out all of the grated potato and
onion. (Moisture is the enemy of fried potatoes.) Discard the juices.

Meanwhile, ready a frying pan (cast iron is perfect for this) with at least ½ inch of oil
and slowly start to heat it over medium heat. Have a baking sheet or two at the ready.

Mix the potatoes, onions, and eggs well with your gloved hands or a spoon. Add
the flour, starting with ¼ cup, and add until the batter will form a ball in your hand,
sticking together.

Test the oil temperature with a tiny bit of latke batter. It should turn golden over
the course of 30 seconds to a minute. If it blackens or smokes, the oil is too hot
and needs to cool on an unheated burner for a minute. To form latkes, place a
clementine-sized (roughly ¾ cup) lump of batter on a cutting board or clean
counter. Flatten it with the palm of your hand while smoothing the edges to make a
5- to 6-inch circle (about the size of a saucer). Narrower and thicker will make a more
creamy-centered latke, while wider and thinner (under ½ inch) will make a crispier
latke. Slide a fish spatula under the latke and place it gently into the oil. If your pan
is large enough, you can fry two at a time. Once you see the edges turning golden
brown, about 3 to 5 minutes, turn it over. Fry the second side for a little less time. You
want it golden but not too dark brown. Take it out of the oil and place on a baking
sheet. Shape and fry the rest of the latkes the same way.

Place the baking sheet of latkes in the oven for about 10 minutes to ensure that
the inside is sufficiently cooked. The latkes will exude oil onto the pan when
the center is cooked enough. If in doubt, cook them a minute or two longer as
undercooked potatoes oxidize and turn black! Serve immediately, with your choice of
accompaniments.

To serve later, allow the latkes to cool before placing them in a covered container
in the refrigerator, where they can last for up to 4 days. To reheat and crisp, fry the
latkes on the stovetop, or place them on a baking sheet in a 350°F oven for about
7 to 10 minutes, until heated through and crispy on the edges.

Grandma Mary, the source of many of the Jewish recipes at BernBaum's, in 1977.

BernBaum's Latkes

We developed our original recipe for latkes after a customer recommended adding potato starch instead of flour as the binder, to keep them gluten-free.

We made 45 latkes at a time using a food processor to grate the potatoes and onions. For this smaller batch, a box grater would work, too. Try to fry the batter within about 20 minutes, before the potatoes oxidize.

The latkes can be served with classic sour cream and applesauce, fancier Crème Fraîche and Apple–Ginger Compote (page 118), lox, capers, Red Onion pickle (page 78), and Crème Fraîche (page 112), or as a side to brisket.

Makes 5 to 6 latkes

1 large egg

1 tablespoon Diamond Crystal kosher salt
    or 1½ teaspoons other kosher salt

½ teaspoon baking powder

¼ teaspoon freshly ground black pepper

5 to 6 medium russet potatoes (about 2½ pounds total), peeled

1 small onion, peeled, halved, root end trimmed*

3 to 4 tablespoons potato starch

Canola oil, for frying

We typically used a yellow onion, but any can work. A red onion will turn bluish-purple.

Preheat the oven to 325°F.

Combine the egg, half of the salt, the baking powder, and pepper in a bowl. Whisk until well blended.

Grate the potatoes and onion on the large holes of a box grater into another large bowl. Or grate them in a food processor with the large grating disk and transfer them to a large bowl. Add the remaining salt and mix well with your gloved hands. Let sit for a few minutes to absorb salt and lose water, but not so long that the potatoes start to turn pinkish.

recipe continues

Set up your potato wringing contraption: Center a clean flour sack towel in a colander set inside another large bowl.

Place a large handful of the potato-onion mixture (no more than 2 cups) in the towel. Gather the edges of the towel together and twist to wring out all the liquid out of the mixture. Unwrap and add the drained mixture to the eggs. Repeat until you have wrung out all of the grated potato and onion. Discard the juices.

Meanwhile, ready a frying pan (cast iron is perfect for this) with at least ½ inch of oil and slowly start to heat it over medium heat. Have a baking sheet or two at the ready.

Mix the potatoes, onions, and eggs well with your gloved hands or a spoon. Add 3 tablespoons of the potato starch and mix well. Add more potato starch until the batter will form a ball in your hand, sticking together.

Test the oil temperature with a tiny bit of the latke batter. It should turn golden over the course of 30 seconds to a minute. If it blackens or smokes, the oil is too hot and needs to cool on an unheated burner for a minute. To form latkes, place a clementine-sized (roughly ¾ cup) lump of batter on a cutting board or clean counter. Flatten it with the palm of your hand while smoothing the edges to make a circle of an even diameter of 5 to 6 inches—narrower and thicker will make a more creamy-centered latke, while wider and thinner (under ½ inch) will make a crispier latke. Slide a fish spatula under the latke and place it gently into the oil. If your pan is large enough, you can fry two at a time. Once you can see the edges turning golden brown, about 3 to 5 minutes, use the spatula to turn it over. Fry the second side for a little less time. You want it golden but not too dark brown. Remove the latke out of the oil and place on a baking sheet. Shape and fry the rest of the latkes the same way.

Place the baking sheet of latkes in the oven for about 10 minutes to ensure that the inside is sufficiently cooked. If in doubt, bake a minute or two longer, as undercooked potatoes turn black! Serve immediately, with your choice of accompaniments.

To serve later, allow the latkes to cool before placing them in a covered container in the refrigerator, where they can last for up to 4 days. To reheat and crisp up, fry on the stovetop, or place them on a baking sheet in a 350°F oven until heated through and crispy on the edges (7 to 10 minutes).

Latkes and Brisket

This is a bit like a Jewish poutine: fried potato base, brisket bits, and caramelized onions, all topped with melted cheese.

Serves 3 or 4

> 4 latkes (page 152 or 155; your choice)
>
> 2 tablespoons canola oil
>
> 2 cups shredded or cubed roasted, braised, or smoked brisket (about 8 ounces)
>
> ½ cup Caramelized Onions (page 48)
>
> 1½ cup grated brick or Swiss cheese
>
> Kosher salt (any brand)
>
> ⅓ cup Crème Fraîche (page 112)
>
> ⅓ cup Carrot-Horseradish Relish (page 86)

Preheat the oven to 350°F.

Place the latkes on a baking sheet and put them on the middle rack of the oven.

Heat an oven-safe sauté pan over medium-high heat. Add the oil to the pan and swirl to coat the bottom. Add the brisket and caramelized onions and stir to mix them. When hot, sprinkle the cheese on top. Place in the oven for about 5 minutes to melt the cheese.

To serve, sprinkle the latkes with salt, and place them on individual plates or a large platter. Serve the cheesy meat mess on the side or atop the latke with crème fraîche and relish.

Latkes and Lox

Fish, pickles, and fried potatoes—a glorious and classic combo.

Serves 4

⅓ cup Crème Fraîche (page 112)

2 tablespoon capers, drained and lightly chopped

¼ cup Red Onion pickles (page 78), drained

8 ounces thinly sliced cold-smoked lox

4 latkes (page 152 or 155—your choice)

Flaky sea salt (such as Maldon)

Place the crème fraîche, capers, and pickled onions in small serving bowls. Arrange the lox on a platter.

If the latkes aren't freshly fried and hot, place them on a baking sheet and reheat in a 350°F oven for 4 to 6 minutes, until hot and crispy. Sprinkle each latke with a pinch of salt and serve the latkes immediately with the accompaniments.

Sandwich Eggs

We opened in a cramped furniture store with an old electric stove, so if we wanted to serve eggs on our bagels, we were going to need to think outside of the stovetop. Thus our sandwich eggs were born, a creamy egg custard baked in a low oven, cut into squares, and layered to create our Bacon, Egg, and Cheese as well as our Romanian Sausage and Egg Bagel. Even when we moved to a professional kitchen, we kept this recipe since it's a great shortcut for making many servings, and the eggs are cooked perfectly. (Necessity is the mother of invention.)

This is most easily mixed with a stick blender, but can be done by hand with a whisk or in a blender jar instead.

Makes enough for 9 sandwiches

> Unsalted butter, room temperature, or nonstick cooking spray
>
> 7 large eggs
>
> ¾ cup half-and-half
>
> 6 tablespoons heavy cream
>
> ½ teaspoon Diamond Crystal kosher salt
> or ¼ teaspoon other kosher salt
>
> 1 teaspoon chopped fresh tender herbs (such as parsley, scallion, dill, chervil, or fennel fronds; optional)

Preheat the oven to 250°F. Grease a 9 × 9-inch baking pan with butter or cooking spray.

Whisk together the eggs, half-and-half, heavy cream, and salt until uniform. Pour into the sprayed pan. Cover with plastic wrap and then foil.

Bake for 20 minutes, reduce to 225°F and bake for 10 to 20 minutes more until almost set—not cooked hard but with a little bit of jiggle in the center. (Once the edges set, it will take about 10 more minutes to fully cook.) Remove from the oven, uncover, and sprinkle with the herbs (if using). Let cool to room temperature.

Cut into thirds in each direction to make 9 squares. Use a fish spatula to lift the pieces out of the pan. Use in sandwiches immediately, or wrap in plastic wrap and store in the refrigerator for later use; they can last for up to 4 days.

BernBaum's Original Bodega–Style Bacon, Egg, and Cheese

We went at least two years before Brett suggested an egg and bacon sandwich. I initially scoffed that it was too boring and definitely not kosher (not that we were kosher, but bacon seemed like pushing it)—but it became our best-selling sandwich from the start. After a while, we replaced the sliced cheese with Maple-Bacon Schmear. Either way, it's a good breakfast standard, which we served with Bread and Butter Pickles and German Mustard.

Makes 4 sandwiches

- 6 pieces bacon, cut in half crosswise
- 4 bagels (page 14 or store-bought), split
- 4 Sandwich Egg squares (page 159)
- 4 slices 2-year-aged cheddar or brick cheese

Preheat the oven to 375°F. Line a platter with paper towels.

Cook the bacon until crisp and fully cooked, 10 to 15 minutes in a baking sheet in the oven, or in a large frying pan on the stovetop. Remove from the oven or stovetop and drain on the paper towels.

Place the bagel halves cut side up on a baking sheet. Put the egg squares on another baking sheet, this one lined with parchment paper. Place both baking sheets in the oven for 3 to 4 minutes, until the bagels are lightly toasted and the eggs are hot. Remove both from the oven.

Top each egg square with 3 pieces of bacon and a slice of cheese and return the baking sheet to the oven. Once the cheese is melted (just a couple of minutes), use a spatula to place an egg square on each of the bagel bottoms. Cover with the bagel top, and slice in half before serving.

BACON, EGG, AND CHEESE 2.0: Omit the slices of cheese. Once the bagels are lightly toasted and the egg-and-bacon combo is atop the bagel bottom, smear the bagel top with a generous dollop of Maple-Bacon Schmear (page 73). Close the sandwiches, cut in half, and serve.

Romanian Sausage

Romanian sausage is a garlicky, herby beef sausage. Serve it as a breakfast sausage or in the Romanian Sausage and Egg Bagel (page 164).

Makes about 6 patties

> 1¼ pounds ground beef
>
> ¼ cup seltzer or club soda
>
> ½ teaspoon baking soda
>
> 4 cloves garlic, peeled and minced
>
> 4½ teaspoons Diamond Crystal kosher salt
>   or 2¼ teaspoons other kosher salt
>
> 1½ teaspoons Hungarian paprika
>
> ½ teaspoon freshly ground black pepper
>
> ¼ cup chopped fresh parsley
>
> 1 teaspoon fresh thyme leaves, minced, or ¼ teaspoon dried thyme
>
> Canola or other neutral oil, for cooking (optional)

MIXING BY HAND: Place the ground beef in a large mixing bowl. Combine the seltzer and baking soda and pour over the meat. Mix it in with a wooden spoon, spatula, or your gloved hand. Add the garlic, salt, paprika, pepper, parsley, and thyme and continue to vigorously stir until it is a uniform mixture and a bit tacky to the touch.

MIXING WITH A STAND MIXER: Place the ground beef in the mixer bowl. Combine the seltzer and baking soda and pour over the meat. Using the paddle attachment, mix on low speed until combined. Stop the mixer and add the garlic, salt, paprika, pepper, parsley, and thyme. Continue to mix on low until uniform and a bit tacky.

Line a baking sheet with wax paper or parchment paper. With a 4-ounce scoop or
½-cup measure, portion the meat into balls. Roll each ball smooth between your
gloved hands, then flatten it into a thin patty. Place on the prepared baking sheet
and repeat with the remaining meat. Cover with plastic wrap and refrigerate for at
least 2 hours or overnight.

If not cooking and serving the sausage immediately, place the patties between
layers of wax paper or parchment paper in a covered container and store in the
refrigerator for up to days.

COOKING IN THE OVEN: Preheat the oven to 350°F. Uncover the baking sheet,
take off the paper with the sausages, remove the sausages from the paper, and
place them back on the pan directly. (Or transfer the sausages from the storage
container to an unlined baking sheet.) Bake for 6 to 8 minutes; the sausages should
be browned and sizzling, and cooked in the center (cut into one to check). Remove
from the oven and serve immediately.

COOKING ON THE STOVETOP: Preheat a large cast-iron or heavy frying pan over
medium-high heat. Add a swirl of oil to coat the bottom of the pan and add as many
sausages as will fit without crowding. (I can fit 3 in my favorite cast-iron pan.) Cook
until the bottom is browned, then turn with a spatula and brown the other side. It
should take about 3 minutes per side. Remove from the pan. Repeat until you've
cooked as many sausages as you need.

Romanian Sausage and Egg Bagel

We served this sandwich with Bread and Butter Pickles and German Mustard.

Makes 4 sandwiches

> 4 bagels (page 14, or store-bought), split
>
> 4 Romanian Sausage patties (page 162)
>
> 4 Sandwich Egg squares (page 159)
>
> ½ cup Horseradish-Dill Schmear (page 73)
>
> 2 cups salad greens, washed and spun dry
>
> Pinch of kosher salt (any brand)
>
> 1 tablespoon Ladolemono (page 225)

Preheat the oven to 400°F.

Place the bagel halves cut side up on a baking sheet. Place sausages and egg squares on another baking sheet lined with parchment paper. Place both baking sheets in the oven for about 5 minutes, until the bagels are lightly toasted and the sausages and eggs are hot. Remove the bagels from the oven if they are done first, then remove the sausages and eggs.

Let cool for a few minutes before amply smearing the schmear on the cut side of the bagel tops. Place a sausage and an egg square on each of the bagel bottoms and close the sandwich. Cut in half and place on serving plates.

Sprinkle the greens with salt and toss with the ladolemono. Place a small handful between the sandwich halves on each plate and serve immediately.

Pat McCoy, her son Willy, and Annika Grove pitching in
to get our Broadway space ready.

Grandpa Skuli Stefanson, no doubt drinking watered-down coffee
from a bone china tea cup, in his trademark suspenders (1987).

Wild Rice Porridge

My Icelandic Grandpa Skuli started every day with a bowl of porridge, to which he attributed his health and mental acuity. We all crave simple porridges from time to time, even if we aren't as committed as the "Reykjavík Rocket." This recipe can be changed up to be a savory breakfast or sweet; see the variations that follow.

Our porridge was a mix of local organic oats, flaked rye, and wild rice. In addition, we made versions with local dried blue corn (also good) and random grains like buckwheat or malted oats—pretty much anything Noreen Thomas and her Doubting Thomas Farms found for us.

Serves 4 to 6

> Kosher salt (any brand)
>
> ⅓ cup wild rice
>
> 1 tablespoon granulated sugar
>
> ¾ cup rolled rye* or coarse-cut rye flour
>
> 1 cup rolled oats
>
> *We bought our rolled rye from Doubting Thomas Farms in Moorhead, Minnesota.*

Bring 1⅓ cups of the water to a simmer over high heat. Add a pinch of salt and the wild rice. Reduce the heat to maintain a simmer, cover, and cook for 30 minutes or until the wild rice is tender but not fully popped. Drain it in a colander or fine mesh strainer and let cool to room temperature. (You can do this up to a few days ahead and refrigerate the wild rice until you're ready to use it.)

Pour 4 cups water into a medium saucepan and bring to a boil. Add the sugar and 1 tablespoon Diamond Crystal kosher salt or 1½ teaspoons other kosher salt. Slowly add the rolled rye while whisking rapidly and continuously. (If you add the rye too quickly, it will clump up into small balls, ruining the consistency of the porridge.) Keep stirring rapidly while you add the oats. Reduce to a simmer and let thicken to desired consistency, about 15 minutes. Stir in the wild rice and cook until it is heated through. Serve as whatever version your heart desires (see the recipes that follow).

You can make this ahead and store it in a closed container in the refrigerator for up to 4 days. To reheat as needed, place a portion in a microwave-safe bowl and microwave on high for 1½ to 2 minutes. To reheat on the stovetop, place ¼ to ½ an inch water in a small saucepan, add the porridge and a smidge of butter and salt, and stir to combine. Heat slowly over medium heat. It is heated throughout when bubbly in the center.

Sweet Porridge

Serves 4 to 6

> 1 batch Wild Rice Porridge (page 167)
> ¾ to 1 cup maple syrup
> ¾ to 1 cup Crème Fraîche (page 112) or sour cream
> 1 to 1½ cups Matzo Granola (page 170)

If the porridge is not freshly made, reheat it according to the directions in the recipe. Spoon the porridge into individual bowls, drizzle with maple syrup, and top with a dollop of crème fraîche and a handful of matzo granola. Easy peasy.

Savory Porridge

This can be done with any assortment of vegetables, even leftover stir-fried vegetables—the possibilities are endless. We tended to use smoked carrot ribbons, roasted beets, and shaved onion in this because they were always available to us. Zhug (page 105) is another first-rate addition.

Serves 4 to 6

> 1 batch Wild Rice Porridge (page 167)
> 1 to 1½ cups chopped sautéed, roasted, or otherwise
>   cooked vegetables, heated
> ¾ to 1 cup Labne (page 76)
> 2 to 3 tablespoons extra virgin olive oil
> 1 to 1½ teaspoons flaky sea salt (such as Maldon)
> 1 to 1½ teaspoons za'atar (optional, but really tasty)

If the porridge is not freshly made, reheat it according to the directions in the recipe. Spoon the porridge into individual bowls, top each with sautéed vegetables and a spoonful of labne. Drizzle with olive oil and sprinkle with the flaky salt and za'atar (if using). Serve immediately.

Matzo Granola

It's maybe gimmicky to make granola with matzo, but the addition of maple syrup and olive oil really complements that blank slate of a cracker. Baking this will make your house smell wonderful. It's also good to snack on.

Makes 6 cups

5 ounces (half a 10-ounce box) matzo, crumbled into roughly 1-inch pieces*

½ cup unsweetened flaked coconut

⅓ cup coarsely chopped raw almonds

2 packed tablespoons light brown sugar

½ teaspoon ground cinnamon

⅛ teaspoon Diamond Crystal kosher salt or a pinch of other kosher salt

½ cup extra virgin olive oil

6 tablespoons maple syrup

1 teaspoon vanilla extract

½ cup chopped mixed dried fruit**

I bash the crackers with my fist while they're still in the wrapping.
**We used a combination of figs, dates, and apricots, but anything will work.*

Preheat the oven to 350°F. Line two baking sheets with parchment paper.

Mix the matzo, coconut, almonds, brown sugar, cinnamon, and salt together in a large bowl. Drizzle evenly with the oil, maple syrup, and vanilla. Toss well so the matzo is well coated with the oil and syrup.

Divide the granola evenly between the prepared baking sheets, spreading it into a single layer. Bake, stirring and turning once or twice, switching the top sheet to the bottom if need be, for 15 to 18 minutes, until the matzo, almonds, and coconut are toasty and golden brown. (Check near the end of the baking time to be sure the granola is not burning—it can go from nicely toasted to overdone very quickly!) Remove from the oven and set aside to cool.

When the granola is cool, stir in the dried fruit. Transfer to an airtight container. This will keep at room temperature for up to 2 weeks.

Soups and Stocks

G ood soup requires good ingredients, tasting at every step of the process, and sometimes only salt and a bit of acid to finish. At BernBaum's, other than the chicken matzo ball we kept the soup choices gluten- and meat-free, as well as mostly dairy-free. We also didn't use recipes. Like salads, soups were born of looking into the cooler to see what surprises we might find—like tomatillos, celery, and brown rice, which made a terrific soup. Sometimes it was a simple vegetable soup, sometimes a fancier puree. My blueprints for soups follow—all are easily modified to fit your refrigerator and your mood.

Myron's Chicken Matzo Ball Soup

Since we were a Jewish deli, I had to figure out how to make a passable matzo ball. Myron Bright (1919–2016) was a local federal judge appointed to the Eighth Circuit by LBJ and a pillar of the Fargo Jewish community. Still working in his nineties, Judge Bright would zoom around town in his wheelchair, pushed by a law clerk. One day early on in my matzo ball apprenticeship, he rolled in and ordered the matzo ball soup. He took a bite and loudly pronounced "Ah, cannonballs." *Oh, no*, I thought. Then, just as authoritatively, he said, "My mother's were like cannonballs."

My Israeli brother-in-law likes his kneidlach (matzo balls) to be as dense and chewy as a piece of licorice, while others like a single fluffy tennis ball floating in their bowl. I've since settled on a light but still toothsome texture closer to floater than sinker, but there are acolytes in both camps. While I no longer serve cannonballs, we named the soup in honor of the bright light that was Myron.

This matzo ball soup starts with a good stock made while poaching the chicken, and adds mirepoix (chunky onion, carrot, and celery, plus other vegetables), the chicken meat, and matzo balls to finish. This is a project, but one that can be easily broken into the individual steps.

You can't have too many hot liquids
at lunch in North Dakota.

Makes 10 to 12 cups stock, about 4 cups (1½ pounds) chicken meat, and 8 to 10 matzo balls; soup serves 4 or 5

Poached Chicken and Chicken Stock

1 tablespoon canola or other neutral oil

½ onion, peeled and coarsely chopped

1 stalk celery, coarsely chopped

1 carrot, peeled and coarsely chopped

1 bay leaf

½ teaspoon black peppercorns

1 sprig fresh thyme or 1 pinch of dried thyme

1 whole chicken (about 3 pounds), rinsed

Place a stock pot over medium-high heat. When hot, add the oil and swirl to coat the bottom. Add the onion, celery, and carrot; the oil will crackle and sizzle if it's at the right temperature. After a minute or two, reduce the heat to medium and leave the vegetables to sweat (cook without coloring), which will be a quieter sizzle.

Give it a few more minutes, until the vegetables deepen in color, then add the bay leaf, peppercorns, thyme, and chicken. Add enough water to cover the chicken by an inch (roughly 3 quarts of water in my stock pot), increase the heat to high, and bring to a simmer. With the pot uncovered, reduce the heat to keep at a low simmer for 45 minutes to an hour, until the chicken is cooked through, 170°F at the thigh, 160°F at the breast (check by inserting an instant-read thermometer). Fish the chicken out of the stock—this is easiest with a large spider, but a pair of slotted spoons or tongs can work, too—let it drain a bit over the stock pot, and place it on a baking sheet or plate to cool. Turn the heat off.

Once the chicken is cool enough to handle, use your gloved hands to pull off the skin in large pieces; set the skin aside to make gribenes (recipe follows). Take the meat off of the carcass: Pull off the leg quarters and strip the meat from the thighs and drumsticks. Set the meat aside on a plate and put the bones back in the stock. Do the same with the wings and breast, adding the bones back to the stock. Make sure you get the oysters (those tasty nuggets of meat on the lower backbone) and other bits of meat off the carcass, then return the rest of the carcass to the stock. Return the stock to the heat and a low simmer for another 45 minutes to an hour.

I don't skim the fat off of the top of the stock—this is the hallmark of a good matzo ball soup. The stock should be a deep golden with some shiny fat droplets on the top.

Fill the sink with cold water and ice. Place a conical strainer in another vessel like another deep pot or very large heatproof plastic container. Pour the chicken stock through the strainer. Discard the solids in the strainer. Place the pot in the ice water to cool rapidly. When cold, cover and store in the refrigerator for up to 4 days; the fat will solidify in a layer on top, and the stock itself may jell.

Tear or chop the meat into roughly 1-inch pieces and set it aside in a closed container in the refrigerator. If not preparing gribenes immediately, place the chicken skin pieces separately on a piece of parchment, and fold it to fit into a separate covered container in the refrigerator. The meat and skin can keep for up to 4 days. If needing to freeze it, place in a resealable plastic bag and freeze for up to a month.

Gribenes and Schmaltz

Gribenes are fried chicken skin pieces that taste almost like bacon. They are beautiful as a garnish for this matzo ball soup or the chicken liver mousse (Chopped Liver, page 74), or on a GLT—BernBaum's version of a BLT. Schmaltz is melted chicken fat and great to cook with. It is especially lovely with starchy vegetables like potatoes.

Skin reserved from Poached Chicken and Chicken Stock

Kosher salt (any brand)

Preheat the oven to 325°F. Line a baking sheet with parchment paper.

Place the skin pieces on the prepared baking sheet. Stretch them out flat so that they aren't crowded or folded over. Sprinkle lightly with salt and bake until very crispy, 15 to 20 minutes.

When they are crispy and browned throughout, remove from the oven. Drain the golden chicken fat into a jar, and let cool. Cover, and refrigerate for up to 1 month for later use. The gribenes can be stored in the refrigerator, in a container lined with a paper towel, for up to a week. Reheat and recrisp in a 350°F oven for 3 to 5 minutes. It's imperative that the gribenes are shatteringly crispy. Otherwise, they will have the texture of undercooked bacon.

recipe continues

Matzo Balls

This is a recipe for matzo balls from plain old matzo meal. The store-bought matzo ball mixes are a reasonable substitute if you don't want to go through this part of the recipe. For those, just follow the package directions to mix, then cover and chill. You can catch up when it's time to form and poach the balls. Please be careful of adding salt if you are using matzo ball mix or store-bought broth.

¾ cup matzo meal

¾ teaspoon baking powder

1½ teaspoons Diamond Crystal kosher salt
   or ¾ teaspoon other kosher salt

4 turns of a pepper mill

2 teaspoons chopped fresh herbs (like parsley, dill, fennel fronds,
   and/or chives; optional, but recommended!)

1 tablespoon minced preserved lemon or grated zest of 1 lemon,
   only for Spring Vegetable Matzo Ball Soup (page 186)

4 large eggs

¼ cup canola oil* and/or Schmaltz** (page 177),
   plus more for greasing (optional)

1 to 2 tablespoons chicken stock or water (optional)

About 6 cups Chicken Stock (page 176) or Vegetable Stock (page 182),
   for poaching***

*If you want to make this vegetarian, replace the schmaltz with oil and water
   and use vegetable stock for poaching.

**If you want to use schmaltz but don't have enough, make up the difference
   with canola oil.

***You can use half stock and half water instead; I don't recommend all water,
   as you need a bit of flavor.

Mix the matzo meal, baking powder, salt, pepper, and herbs (if using) in a large bowl. Use a whisk to mix them completely. If making these for Spring Vegetable Matzo Ball Soup (page 186), add the preserved lemon.

In another bowl, whisk together the eggs and oil. Pour this over the matzo meal mixture and mix well with a spoon. The right consistency is gloopy but not runny. If it feels too stiff, add a tablespoon or two of stock or water. Place plastic wrap over the surface of the batter and refrigerate for at least 30 minutes, up to 6 hours. Do not mix a day ahead; the matzo balls will tend to get craggy and sometimes explode while you're poaching them.

Line a baking sheet with parchment paper or grease it with oil or schmaltz. Use a small scoop (less than an ounce) or spoon to portion the matzo ball batter onto the prepared baking sheet. Use your hands to round them into balls the size of a large gumball. You should have between 8 and 10 matzo balls. Set aside until the poaching liquid is ready.

Heat the poaching liquid in a stock pot or large saucepan to a simmer. (The stock should fill two-thirds of the pot at most.) Drop a test matzo ball into the simmering stock. It should drop into the stock, then rise to the top within a minute. If it doesn't, your stock might not be hot enough. Increase heat before adding the rest of the matzo balls. Once all of the matzo balls are in the stock, cover with parchment or waxed paper, and then a pot lid. Reduce heat to a low simmer for 15 minutes before checking them. (Do not let them boil, as they will explode into blobs.) Turn off the heat and let them sit in the hot stock, covered, for an additional 15 minutes, which is usually a perfect amount of time to cook them through to the center. To check, cut one in half. If done, there won't be any dry spots in the center, and the texture of the ball will be the same throughout. It will have doubled in size as well. Use a spider or slotted spoon to fish them out of the stock and place on a clean baking sheet to cool.

You can make the matzo balls and refrigerate them in a covered container up to 3 days ahead of finishing the soup, although they have a lighter texture on the first day. Strain and refrigerate the stock to use in the final soup.

recipe continues

Chicken Matzo Ball Soup

At the restaurant, we kept the soup separate from the matzo balls until we heated them for service, as the matzo balls would absorb all of the stock—which tastes good, it's just not soup.

Serves 4 to 6, makes 2½ quarts

2 tablespoons canola or other neutral oil

½ yellow onion, peeled, root and stem ends trimmed, finely diced

1 carrot, peeled and cut in ½-inch dice or slices

1 parsnip, peeled and cut in ½-inch dice or slices

1 small rutabaga or turnip,* peeled and cut in ½-inch dice (optional)

2 stalks celery, cut in ¼-inch dice or slices

7 cups Chicken Stock (preferably homemade, page 176),
  or stock plus water

Half of the reserved chicken meat** (from Poached Chicken, page 176)
  or 2 cups (about 10 ounces) boneless, skinless rotisserie chicken meat

1 tablespoon Diamond Crystal kosher salt
  or 1½ teaspoons other kosher salt***

5 turns of a pepper mill

2 tablespoons chopped fresh herbs (thyme, oregano, parsley, dill—
  whatever you have on hand) or 1 teaspoon of dried herbs (optional)

Splash of sherry vinegar, or red or white wine vinegar

1 batch Matzo Balls (page 178)

Minced fresh herbs (fennel fronds, dill, parsley,
  and/or scallion greens), for garnish

Gribenes (page 177), for garnish (optional)

*As a Jewish friend says, a bold choice. If not using, add another carrot and
  parsnip each.

**Save the rest for chicken salad or another batch of soup.

***If you are using store-bought broth, bouillon cubes plus water, or matzo balls
  from a packaged mix, be careful as those may already be sufficiently salted!

Heat a soup pot over medium-high heat. Add the oil and swirl to cover the bottom. Add the onion, carrots, parsnip, and rutabaga (if using). Cook the vegetables at a nice, steady sizzle and crackle. After about 5 minutes, add the celery. Continue at a nice pace for another 3 to 5 minutes, until the vegetables look cooked.

Add the stock and bring to a simmer. Add the chicken. Season with the salt, pepper, herbs (if using), and vinegar to taste. If serving immediately, drop in the matzo balls and simmer for 3 to 5 minutes, until heated through. Ladle the soup, vegetables, chicken, and matzo balls into 4 or 5 large bowls. Garnish with the minced herbs and the gribenes (if using).

The soup—without the matzo balls—can be cooled and refrigerated in a covered container for up to 3 days. Add and reheat the matzo balls just before serving, and garnish as above.

Vegetable Stock

My ideas of acceptable stock vegetables were shaped by European cooking school instructors over twenty-five years ago. I know that the culinary world has changed since then, but I haven't been able to shake this habit. I am horrified by the addition of bell pepper scraps, but it is a response based on habit rather than knowledge. Think about what a vegetable tastes like when cooked and if that flavor will add to or detract from the final product, whether it's in a finished soup or a base stock for another dish.

We generally used vegetable scraps (without the peel) from all of the standard mirepoix vegetables—onion, garlic, carrot, celery, parsnip, fennel, mushroom, and parsley stems—modifying the basic recipe in ways that made sense for us and tasted good. If in the mood for something decidedly un-Nordic, for example, we might have added dried chiles and cilantro stems to the stock.

At home, I save up vegetable scraps in a resealable gallon-size plastic bag in the freezer, and make stock when necessary. This isn't as good as freshly cooked, but it does make a serviceable stock.

Makes about 3 quarts

> 1 tablespoon canola or other neutral oil
>
> 4 cups clean vegetable scraps *or*
>   1 yellow onion, peeled, root and stem ends trimmed, chopped
>
> 1 carrot, peeled, chopped
>
> 1 parsnip, peeled, chopped
>
> 1 stalk celery, chopped
>
> ½ fennel bulb, chopped or sliced ¼ inch across,
>   or four 8-inch fronds, chopped (about 1 cup)

Heat a stock pot over medium-high heat. Add the oil and swirl to cover the base of the pot. Add the vegetables and sweat them (cook without coloring), stirring, for 3 to 5 minutes, until they glisten and are partially cooked. Add 3 quarts water and bring to a simmer. Adjust the heat to maintain a simmer, uncovered, for 20 to 30 minutes.

Strain out and discard the solids. Let the stock cool to room temperature before dividing it into covered containers and refrigerating or freezing it.

The stock keeps for up to a week in the refrigerator or a month frozen. Freezing in smaller, portion-sized containers, ice cube trays, or heavy-duty resealable plastic bags is helpful when you make a large batch at once like this. There's nothing better than finding great ingredients already in your freezer!

Joe Swegarden, a fellow chef, and Zoe Absey at a BernBaum's dinner.

Vegetarian Matzo Ball Soup

Two years ago, we added a vegetarian matzo ball option to the menu. This version is so good, teeming with herbs and earthy root vegetables, you won't miss the schmaltz.

Serves 4 or 5

1 tablespoon canola or other neutral oil

½ small yellow onion, peeled, root and stem ends trimmed,
cut in ¼-inch dice

1 carrot, peeled, cut in ½-inch dice or slices

1 parsnip, peeled and cut in ½-inch dice or slices

1 small rutabaga or turnip, peeled and cut in ½-inch dice (optional)

¼ fennel bulb, cut in ¼-inch dice or slices across,
or two 8-inch fronds, chopped (about ½ cup)

1 stalk celery, cut in ¼-inch dice or slices

2 teaspoons Hawaij Spice Mix (page 92)

6 cups Vegetable Stock (preferably homemade, page 182) or water

1½ teaspoons Diamond Crystal kosher salt
or ¾ teaspoon other kosher salt*

¼ teaspoon freshly ground black pepper

Splash of sherry vinegar or fresh lemon juice

4 or 5 leaves lacinato kale,** tough stems removed
and leaves sliced into ribbons (about 1 cup)

1 batch Matzo Balls (page 178)***

1 tablespoon minced fresh herbs (parsley, dill, fennel fronds,
and/or scallions)

*If you are using store-bought broth, bouillon cubes and water, or matzo balls
from a packaged mix, be careful as those may already be sufficiently salted!

**Lacinato kale is also known as Tuscan kale or dinosaur kale. If substituting
another kale, be sure to stem before slicing the leaves.

***To keep the soup vegetarian, make the matzo balls with canola oil and water,
and poach them in vegetable stock.

Heat a soup pot over medium-high heat. Add the oil and swirl to coat the bottom. Add the onions, carrots, parsnips, and rutabaga (if using), and sweat the vegetables (cook without browning) until the onion is translucent. Add the fennel and celery and continue to cook for a few more minutes, taking care not to brown the vegetables Add the hawaij and stir to coat the vegetables while toasting the spices a bit. Add the stock and bring to a simmer. Season with the salt, pepper, and vinegar or lemon juice to taste.

Add the kale. Bring the soup back to a simmer and add the matzo balls. Simmer until the matzo balls are heated through, 3 to 5 minutes. Ladle into bowls, garnish with the herbs, and serve immediately.

If not serving immediately, cool to room temperature before adding the kale. Refrigerate in a covered container for up to 4 days, until you're ready to serve. Bring to a simmer over medium-high heat, add and heat the matzo balls, then serve, garnished with the herbs.

Spring Vegetable Matzo Ball Soup

For a Passover dinner a few years back, we made this verdant soup with preserved lemon and herby matzo balls. Yes, you can add delicious bits to matzo balls!

Serves 4 to 6, makes a little over 2 quarts of soup

 1 tablespoon canola oil or other neutral oil

 1 medium leek, white part only, root end trimmed,
  thoroughly washed, cut in ¼-inch dice

 1 clove garlic, peeled and minced

 ½ cup sorrel leaves, washed and sliced into ¼-inch chiffonade*

 ½ fennel bulb with fronds, cut in ¼-inch dice

 1 stalk celery, sliced across ¼-inch thick

 1 tablespoon minced mixed fresh herbs (parsley, dill, fennel fronds,
  and/or scallion green)

 5 cups Vegetable Stock (preferably homemade, page 182) or water

 1½ teaspoons Diamond Crystal kosher salt
  or ¾ teaspoon other kosher salt**

 ¼ teaspoon freshly ground black pepper

 Splash of sherry vinegar or fresh lemon juice

 8 ounces asparagus, woody ends snapped off,
  sliced into 1-inch lengths (about 1½ cups cut asparagus)

 3 ounces sugar snap or snow peas, julienned (cut into matchsticks)
  or cut in half lengthwise (about 1 cup)

 1 batch Matzo Balls (page 178)***

*If you can't find sorrel, add the zest of 1 lemon.

**If you are using store-bought broth, bouillon cubes and water, or matzo balls from a packaged mix, be careful as those may already be sufficiently salted.

***To keep the soup vegetarian, make the matzo balls with canola oil and water, and poach them in vegetable stock. Be sure to add the optional herbs and preserved lemon!

Heat a soup pot over medium-high heat. Add the oil and swirl to coat the bottom. Add the leek and garlic and sweat the vegetables (cook without browning) until the leek is translucent. Add the sorrel, fennel, and celery and continue to cook for a few more minutes, until the sorrel liquefies. Add the herbs and stir to coat all the vegetables. Add the stock and bring to a simmer. Season to taste with salt, pepper, and vinegar or lemon juice.

Add the asparagus, peas, and matzo balls. Simmer until the matzo balls are heated through and the vegetables are barely tender, about 3 to 5 minutes. Ladle into bowls and serve immediately.

If not serving immediately, cool to room temperature before adding the asparagus and peas. Refrigerate in a covered container for up to 4 days, until you're ready to serve. Bring to a simmer over medium-high heat, then add the matzo balls, heat them, and serve.

Silky Beet Borscht

A smooth soup just seems so elegant, but it can be as simple as pulling out your blender after making a simple vegetable soup. Here is a smooth borscht recipe—one that I serve hot or cold depending on the season.

Serves 4 to 6, makes 2 quarts

> 1 tablespoon canola or neutral oil
>
> 1 small onion, peeled, root and stem ends trimmed, cut in ¼-inch dice
>
> 1 shallot, peeled, root and stem ends trimmed, minced
>
> 1 tablespoon minced fresh dill or ½ teaspoon dried dill weed,
>   plus more to taste (optional)
>
> ½ teaspoon caraway seeds (optional)
>
> ¼ teaspoon celery seeds (optional)
>
> 2 stalks celery, cut in ¼-inch dice
>
> 1 carrot, peeled and cut in ½-inch dice
>
> 1 medium potato (like Yukon Gold or red), peeled and cut in ½-inch dice
>
> 2 or 3 medium beets (about 1¼ pounds total), root and stem ends
>   trimmed, peeled, and diced*
>
> 5 to 6 cups water, or 1 quart Vegetable Stock
>   (preferably homemade, page 182) plus 1 to 2 cups water
>
> 1 tablespoon Diamond Crystal kosher salt
>   or 1½ teaspoons other kosher salt
>
> ½ teaspoon freshly ground black pepper
>
> 1 teaspoon apple cider vinegar
>
> Crème Fraîche (page 112), for serving (optional)
>
> Minced fresh herbs or herb oil, for serving (optional)

You can use either red or golden beets; if using golden, roast them before peeling and dicing, to get the best color.

Heat a soup pot over medium-high heat. Add the oil and swirl to coat the bottom. Let it warm; it will look shimmery when ready. Add the onion and shallot and sweat them (cook without coloring) for a few minutes. Add the dill and the caraway and/ or celery seeds (if using). Add the celery and carrot and continue to cook, stirring occasionally, for a few minutes, until they deepen in color and are partially cooked. Stir in the potato and beets.

When the potato and beets have had a few minutes to meld with the other vegetables, add the water and bring to a simmer. Maintain a low simmer for about 30 minutes, until the beets and potatoes are soft. Remove from the heat.

The easiest way to puree the soup is with a stick blender, directly in the pot. You can also use a food mill or jar blender. To use a food mill, fit it with the finest plate and place over a clean saucepan. Pour the soup in a little at a time. Discard any solids that remain in the mill. If using a jar blender, either cool the soup completely first, or only fill the jar half full, then repeat with the rest of the soup.

Once the soup is pureed, add the salt, pepper, and vinegar.

To serve the soup cold, or if you won't be serving it immediately, pour it into a container, cover, and refrigerate until chilled. Just before serving the cold soup, taste it and adjust the seasoning with more salt, pepper, and/or vinegar, and a bit more fresh dill, if you like. Garnish with crème fraîche and more herbs, if you wish.

To serve hot, bring the soup just to a simmer over medium heat. Adjust the seasoning if necessary and add a bit more fresh dill, if you like. Garnish as above.

The borscht will keep in a covered container in the refrigerator for up to 4 days

Cold Summer Borscht

This is another recipe brought to us by former BernBaum's chef Paul Perez. Although cold soup is not a Midwestern convention like hotdish is, we had some luck selling it during our insanely hot summer months. Even when it is 100°F outside, though, it still takes a nudge to get a Fargoan to try a cold soup. In fact, we sold mainly chili and Matzo Ball Soup all summer despite our efforts to diversify.

This is like a beet salad that you can eat with a spoon. I think of this soup as a first course, or to be served with a hummus platter or large green salad, not as a meal in itself. But do what sounds good to you. Season a cold soup carefully, as it will dissolve salt more slowly.

Makes 4 to 6 generous cups

> 1½ pounds red beets, scrubbed, root and stem ends trimmed
>
> 2 tablespoons + 1 teaspoon Diamond Crystal kosher salt
>   or 3½ teaspoons other kosher salt
>
> 1 English cucumber, peeled, seeded, and diced ¼ inch
>
> ¾ cup sliced scallions (green and white parts)
>
> ¼ cup minced fresh dill
>
> 3 cups whole milk yogurt, plus more for garnish (optional)
>
> 4 or 5 turns of a pepper mill
>
> Crème Fraîche (page 112), for garnish (optional)
>
> Minced fresh herbs, for garnish (optional)
>
> Beet chips, such as Terra (optional)

Place the beets in a large soup pot and cover with water. Add 1 tablespoon of the Diamond Crystal or 1½ teaspoons other kosher salt and bring to a simmer. Cook until the beets are tender and a fork or small paring knife can easily make it to the center of the beet, 20 to 25 minutes. Remove from the heat and allow them to cool in the liquid. (This should take 30 to 45 minutes.)

Drain the beets, reserving the liquid for the soup. Peel the beets; you can do this easily by rubbing off the skin with a towel that you don't mind dyeing purple, or with your gloved hands. Shred the beets on the large holes of a box grater into a large bowl.

Mix the cucumber, scallions, dill, and yogurt into the beets. Thin with the reserved cooking liquid until it is the consistency you like. (I like a chunky soup.) Season with the remaining salt and the pepper.

Transfer the soup to a covered container and refrigerate for up to 4 days. When you're ready to serve, check the seasoning and adjust accordingly. You can garnish it with yogurt or crème fraîche, a sprinkling of herbs, and/or beet chips (your choice).

Late Summer Bread and Tomato Soup

In 1990, I spent a college semester in Spain. A decade later, I became the founding chef at Cobras and Matadors, a popular tapas restaurant in Los Angeles, so Spanish flavors are comforting to me. This is my very simple version of gazpacho, which I always pull out when there are too many beautiful garden tomatoes. To be completely truthful, I don't measure any of the ingredients, but just throw them together, with some sherry vinegar and extra virgin olive oil to finish the following day. But since this is a cookbook, the recipe is below.

Serves 4 to 6, makes 2 quarts

1 medium onion, peeled, root and stem ends trimmed, halved

5 to 7 medium tomatoes,* between 1½ to 2 pounds total

1 cucumber,* peeled, quartered lengthwise, and seeded,
   roughly 8 ounces

1 bell pepper (any color), stemmed and seeded

1 small fresh chile (like jalapeño or serrano), stemmed,
   seeded if you prefer

2 cloves garlic, peeled and smashed with the side of a knife blade

2 cups torn pieces stale bread, with the crust,**
   about 6 to 7 ounces of bread

¼ cup sherry vinegar

½ cup extra virgin olive oil, plus more for garnish (optional)

2 teaspoons Diamond Crystal kosher salt or 1 teaspoon other kosher salt

4 turns of a pepper mill

1 teaspoon urfa biber flakes or Aleppo pepper

½ teaspoon smoked paprika

Minced fresh herbs (parsley, oregano and chives are good ones),
   for garnish (optional)

Flaky sea salt (like Maldon), for garnish (optional)

The soup will be best if you use tomatoes and cucumber fresh from the garden.

**We most often used focaccia because we always had day-old on hand, but
   any French- or Italian-style white bread will do.*

Chop the onion, tomatoes, cucumber, bell pepper, and chile. Combine them in a large bowl with the garlic, bread, vinegar, and olive oil. Stir to mix well. Cover the bowl or transfer to a covered container and refrigerate overnight.

FINISHING IN A BLENDER: Pour 1 cup water into the blender jar and top with as much of the tomato-bread mixture as will fit. Blend until smooth. Pour two-thirds of the puree into a clean bowl and fill the blender jar with a second portion of the tomato-bread mixture. Blend again until smooth. Again pour out two-thirds and continue until you have used all of the tomato-bread mix.

FINISHING IN A FOOD PROCESSOR: Fill the food processor bowl with as much of the tomato-bread mixture as will fit and 1 cup water. Process until smooth and pour two-thirds into a clean bowl and fill the food processor with a second portion of the tomato-bread mixture. Process again until smooth. Again pour out two-thirds and continue until you have used all of the tomato-bread mix.

I like to strain the soup through a medium-mesh strainer after pureeing to make it even smoother, but this is optional.

Season with the salt, black pepper, urfa biber or Aleppo pepper, and smoked paprika. Serve immediately with your choice of garnishes. Or refrigerate in a covered container for up to 4 days; stir well before serving.

MD Chili

This recipe is courtesy of My Dad, David Baumgardner, who is also a Medical Doctor (hence the name!). I have happily eaten more of it than any other soup in the world. He volunteered his time to make 7-gallon batches at BernBaum's during the winter, and it sold out quickly, thanks to his legions of fans—as a doctor, cook, and friend. Dad also attempted to buy take-out quarts of a product he had made for free. (If only we could get the rest of the world to do this.) We served it with a dollop of Crème Fraîche and pickled onions.

As teens in the 1980s, my sisters and I remember a process of opening a lot of cans and jars into an army green Crock-Pot, because you really had to be a hippie from California back then to soak beans. For BernBaum's, Dad learned to use dried beans, and there was a fair amount of hand-dicing of onions and garlic. Because he is first and foremost a doctor, Dad refuses to let any meat fat stay in the soup and distrusts my assertion that fat is flavor. Luckily, MD Chili is flavorful without the fat, and his way might keep you out of the doctor's office. I also like to spoon it over a bit of brick or cheddar cheese in my bowl to make a cheesy chili.

> *To get 4 cups cooked pinto beans, soak 1½ cups dried beans overnight in at least 4 cups water. The next morning, drain and place them in a saucepan. Add ½ teaspoon baking soda, 1 bay leaf, 2 smashed garlic cloves (no need to peel), and 4 cups fresh water. Bring to a gentle boil, reduce heat to maintain a low simmer, cover the pan and cook until tender, 40 to 60 minutes. Drain in a colander. Remove the bay leaf and garlic before using.*

Makes about 3½ quarts; serves 6 to 8

1 pound extra lean (93% lean) ground beef*

½ pound ground pork

4 tablespoons ground cumin

5 tablespoons chili powder

1 tablespoon + 2 teaspoons Diamond Crystal kosher salt
   or 2½ teaspoons other kosher salt

¼ cup canola or other neutral oil

2 medium onions, peeled, root and stem ends trimmed,
   diced small (about 2 cups)

6 cloves garlic, peeled and minced (approximately 2 tablespoons)

1½ cups chili sauce (such as Heinz)

5 cups canned whole tomatoes with their juices,** pureed or mashed

4 cups drained cooked pinto beans or drained and rinsed canned beans

1 cup juice from Fresh Pepper Harissa (page 110) or water

2 to 3 tablespoons chopped bittersweet chocolate (70% cacao or higher)***

1 teaspoon Aleppo pepper flakes

Optional additional spices: ½ teaspoon ground cinnamon,
   1 teaspoon sweet paprika, 1 teaspoon smoked paprika

*Bison works well, too, without fat to skim.
**Dad prefers San Marzano tomatoes.
***Dad's surprise ingredient!

Mix the beef, pork, 2 tablespoons of the cumin, 3 tablespoons of the chili powder, and 1 tablespoon Diamond Crystal or 1 ½ teaspoons other salt together in a large bowl with your gloved hands or a wooden spoon. Work the spices into the meat. Set aside.

Heat a Dutch oven or other wide pot over medium-high heat. Add 2 tablespoons of the oil and swirl to coat the bottom. When the oil is hot and shimmering, lower the heat to medium, add the onions and garlic, and sweat them (cook without coloring) for 3 to 5 minutes, until soft and translucent. Pour the onions and garlic into a small bowl to reserve for later.

If vegetables are cooking too fast when you sweat them, covering the pot will ensure that they cook without browning.

recipe continues

Swirl the second glug of oil in the bottom of the pan and add the meat mixture. Mash it up with a spatula or wooden spoon and move it around to ensure that is broken into small pieces and all of it cooks. Once it is all browned, about 7 to 10 minutes, if you are a retired health professional, you may choose to drain the fat out of the pan before you proceed.

Add back the onions and garlic. Add the chili sauce, tomatoes, beans, and harissa juice. Bring to a simmer and cook for 30 to 40 minutes, stirring every so often to make sure that the tomatoes aren't burning to the bottom of the pot. (Lowering the heat to low and covering the pot will also ensure that it is cooking gently.)

Add the chocolate, Aleppo pepper, the remaining salt, and the remaining 2 tablespoons each of cumin and chili powder, as well as any of the optional spices that sound good to you. Continue to simmer for another 30 minutes.

You can serve the chili immediately, but it benefits from a day of refrigeration. Remove from the heat and cool (by placing the cooking pot in a sink full of ice water or a snowbank) to room temperature before refrigerating. Transfer to a covered container and refrigerate of up to 5 days. Reheat gently over low heat. You can also portion it into meal-size containers and freeze for up to a month.

Salads and Dressings

Although this may be a symptom of my declining faculties, I limit total salad elements to no more than five or six, choosing from these very general categories: greens, grains or rice, protein, fruits and/or vegetables, pickles, crunch, and dressing. This way, my salads run the gamut of flavor and texture but don't sacrifice simplicity.

GREENS
PICKLES
GRAINS
RICE
BABY LETTUCES
CABBAGE
SHREDDED KALE
RED ONIONS
CAPER BERRIES
OAT GROATS
BULGUR WHEAT
LEMON DILL VINAIGRETTE
DRESSING
WALNUTS
BEETS
RADISH
FETA
POACHED EGG
SMOKED SALMON
CUCUMBER
STRAWBERRIES
CRUNCH
PROTEIN
FRUITS & VEG

BernBaum's Fundamentals of Salad Making

Salads aren't like wedding cakes. Salads are constructed in loose layers, rather than strictly engineered. My mantra is: Have fun, don't be precious or overthink it, and make it something you really want to eat—not just should eat. To that end, here are the foundational building blocks that I followed at BernBaum's.

Greens

While in cooking school, I externed at Chez Panisse in Berkeley, which shaped my approach to cooking in general and to salads in particular. Chez Panisse was founded by Alice Waters, a chef and food philosopher who has inspired at least two generations of cooks to seek better, sustainably grown ingredients. She also founded The Edible Schoolyard, an organization dedicated to transforming the health of children through hands-on learning in the kitchen, garden, and cafeteria.

One important thing I learned from my time at Chez Panisse is to be discriminating and gentle with greens. Choose greens that have been cared for, preferably buying them from the grower or a reputable market. I tend toward organic greens, as I like the flavor better. I don't recommend premade mixes of different lettuces; there is always one type of lettuce that is bruised or rotting, and sorting through the greens is depressing. (Trust me—I've done it a bunch.)

For our purposes, I separate tender greens (baby lettuces, baby spinach and kale, arugula, butter lettuce, and even tender herbs) from sturdy greens (grown-up spinach, kales, beet greens, and cabbages). Romaine is somewhere between the two, as is frisée. Tender greens add delicate flavors and textures, but they spoil quickly and need a delicate touch in washing and dressing. Sturdy greens have more assertive flavors, hold up to more vigorous handling, and last longer. Their deeper colors also belie a rich nutrient base. My husband and son would never eat a kale salad, so I recognize that sturdy greens have their haters—but using these techniques should help to convert even the most vitamin-averse among us.

Also, an important footnote: Always salt your bare greens before you dress the salad. Just salting the dressing is never enough.

WASHING GREENS AND HERBS
If you have spent the time to find beautiful greens—especially if you live in North Dakota in the winter—continue their loving care by washing them gently.

If you have whole heads, core them and separate the leaves. Fill a large bowl at least four times the volume of the greens with cold water and drop them in. Swish the greens in the water for a minute, allowing dirt and bugs to drop to the bottom of the bowl. Gently lift out the greens and place in a colander to drip dry for 5 to 10 minutes. You can also use a standard salad spinner to spin them dry, taking care not to fill the spinner bowl more than halfway. Layer the greens on a clean kitchen towels or paper towels and seal them in a plastic bag or closed container.

PRE-GAMING STURDY GREENS

For those days when you don't want to masticate as much as a cow, I recommend tenderizing sturdy greens in one of the following ways: a quick cure; wilting; or a chiffonade.

Grains and Rice

Cooked grains and rice are a great way to make a salad into a super healthy meal, adding bulk, fiber, and protein. Some of my regional favorites are available through Red River Harvest Cooperative. I love the oat groats grown by Doubting Thomas Farms and wild rice from Red Lake Nation Foods or the White Earth Wild Rice Program, but lots of things can work for your salad—from bulgur to couscous to pasta, and many varieties of rice.

Proteins

Eggs, an interesting cheese, and bits of meat easily up your salad game to make it a main dish.

EGGS

At our previous restaurant, Green Market, we would "put an egg on it" when we didn't know how to finish a recipe. It was half *Portlandia* joke, half truth.

CHEESE

You can grate semi-soft to hard cheeses with a Microplane, shred them, dice, julienne (cut into matchsticks), or shave them with a y-peeler. Softer cheeses, you can cut in wedges or smear on the plate. I am partial to a smear of soft blue cheese or Labne (page 76) on the outside edge of a salad.

MEAT AND FISH

Keep these as a grace note—a smattering of smoked fish, a bit of shredded brisket, or a few lardons. For hot-smoked fish like trout or whitefish, take the skin off of the fillet, debone it (taking care to get all of the feathery pin bones), and crumble with your gloved hands. For cold-smoked or cured fish, thin slices are very sexy in a composed salad platter, or you can also julienne it (cut into matchsticks) for a chopped salad.

Vegetables and Fruit

We tried to keep our fruit and vegetable choices seasonal. In the Upper Midwest, there are some early summer gifts, like radishes and juneberries, but the real bounty is from July to October. Not much grows around here in the winter, but we used locally grown storage vegetables—squash, root vegetables, and potatoes—well into the next year.

If you use produce that is in season your cooking will be diverse and special throughout the year. I look forward to asparagus season—spring—because I only use it for those three to four months, which is still three times longer than the local season. Fresh tomatoes are thrilling because I only use them when they are locally available in late summer. While I am grateful for coffee and olive oil year round, I appreciate the better taste, higher quality, and cheaper cost of in-season produce that hasn't had to travel from California or Peru.

Starting around April, I include asparagus, peas, and pea shoots, and morels from outside the region, because we are desperate for fresh at that point. May and early June allow for some local hoop house or greenhouse-grown items like greens and sometimes even tomatoes. Later June adds local greens, radishes, local pea shoots, maybe the first cuttings of local asparagus and ramps and lovely juneberries. July heats it up with

WINTER
SPRING
EARLY SUMMER
LATE SUMMER
EARLY FALL
LATE FALL

beans—oh how I love romano beans and string beans—onions, summer squash, and other local berries. August and September are usually an embarrassment of riches—everything that can grow here is harvested. It is also the time of year that I wish I canned for real. Once we get into late fall, we are back to potatoes, onions, winter squash, apples, wild plums, beets, carrots, turnips, and parsnips. By December, I am again grateful for global trade routes, and include citrus and tropical fruits from elsewhere in my rotation. BernBaum's didn't have a purely locavore agenda—we broke our menu up with items from all over the world while trying to support the good growers, ranchers, and stockists in our neck of the woods.

Most vegetables can be put in salads raw, as long as they are thinly sliced, diced, shaved, spiralized, or wedged.

A favorite tool for thinly slicing or cutting perfect matchsticks without a ton of practice is a Benriner mandoline—an adjustable Japanese hand-held slicer with multiple blades. I am also quite enamored of my spiralizer, which makes a raw beet or rutabaga salads look otherworldly.

Cutting into wedges or halves is a good choice for tender and roundish fruits, like berries and plums, and cooked vegetables like beets and potatoes.

For citrus (oranges or grapefruits), I recommend the art of the supreme—a French technique in which you cut off the top and bottom of the fruit, stand it on one end, then use the knife to separate the peel (including the white pith) from the flesh in strips from top to bottom. When you have completely peeled the fruit, slice along both sides of the membranes between the segments to free the flesh of the fruit. You will end up with crescents of citrus without any white pith, peel, or membrane.

Blanching is a good technique for brightly colored vegetables that require a bit of tenderizing, like snap peas, beans, and asparagus. Use a large pot (larger than seems necessary) that will keep the water closer to a boil as you add vegetables—a stock pot is perfect. Fill the pot two-thirds with water and bring to a boil over high heat. I add 1 tablespoon salt per 4 quarts water; this helps the water maintain a boil after I add the vegetables, and adds to their flavor. Once you add your vegetables, most should

SUPREME

take 30 to 60 seconds to blanche after the water returns to a boil, depending upon size and density (larger and denser takes longer) and how crunchy you like your vegetables. Lift them out with a spider (an awesome straining tool available at any Asian market) and place them in a bowl of ice water. Don't skip this step as it is the secret to a brightly colored vegetable. When they're cool, after 5 minutes or so, drain and use in a salad, or store in a closed container in the refrigerator to use later.

You can apply this method to denser vegetables, too. I generally cook potatoes, beets, turnips, and other root vegetables until they are just cooked through and it is not necessary to shock them in a bowl of ice water. Just drain, cool, and use.

I also like roasted vegetables in a salad. I cut vegetables in a roll cut to get many facets for caramelization. Carrots and other cylinders are perfect for this. To roll cut, lay the vegetable on the cutting board. Make a diagonal slice off the bottom, give the vegetable a quarter-turn, and cut on the diagonal through the flat surface created by the previous cut. Turn the vegetable a quarter-turn again and cut on the diagonal again. Repeat until you are at the top end of the vegetable. I have used roasted fruit such as citrus slices, apple wedges, and tomato in salads on occasion, which intensifies the fruit flavor and can be a nice complement if you are using a soft cheese.

Toss the cut vegetables with oil, season with salt and whatever else you would like, and spread on a baking sheet. Roast in a hot oven, around 400°F, until browned around the edges and the texture you would like. Roasted asparagus will take a few minutes; beets or other dense vegetables will take more like 12 to 15 minutes.

ROLL CUT

Pickles

I am never one to limit the brine in any dish. For example, I like a quick-pickled slaw of cabbage, pepper and carrot to toss with greens and feta. Store-bought pickles like cornichons, olives, and capers also add brightness to salads—capers or olives in a vinaigrette-dressed potato salad is classic. For pickle recipes you might try, see pages 77 to 82.

Crunch

Crunchy textures in a salad are important to offset the more tender ingredients and give the dish some heft. You can bring the crunch with raw fruits or veggies, or with ingredients like toasted, candied, or spiced nuts, a savory granola, croutons, or toasted breadcrumbs. At BernBaum's, we used smashed bagel chips for a twist on Fattoush, a Lebanese bread salad.

La Pièce de Résistance (Dressing)

Dressing is such an easy item to master—it can be as simple as our Ladolemono (page 225) or as complex as you want to make it. I have found that a small stick blender is a godsend for emulsifying dressings—that is, creating a dressing where the ingredients stay in suspension, like bottled versions. You can also use a whisk or blender. Whisks make beautiful broken (unemulsified) dressings and also dressings with ingredients that you don't want pureed.

Another way to keep dressings emulsified or evenly mixed is to add a pinch of xanthan gum before adding the oil. Xanthan gum is readily available in the natural food section of most grocery stores. It is a powerful thickening agent, so you only need a pinch (less than $\frac{1}{8}$ teaspoon) for a pint of dressing. One package of Bob's Red Mill xanthan gum lasted us for gallons and gallons of recipes.

Most of these recipes will make a little over a cup of dressing, all of which will stay perfectly tasty in the refrigerator for up to a week (even longer if it's a vinaigrette). If I am going to the trouble of making dressing, why not have extra for tomorrow's lunch?

Quick-Cured Greens

Makes about 2 cups

> 2 cups torn or chopped sturdy greens,
>   stemmed if the stems are thick and fibrous
>
> ½ teaspoon Diamond Crystal kosher salt
>   or ¼ teaspoon other kosher salt
>
> ½ teaspoon granulated sugar

Place the greens in a medium bowl. Mix the salt and sugar together and sprinkle over the greens. Work the mix into the leaves using your gloved hand. Cover and let sit in the refrigerator for at least half an hour or up to a day before adding to your salad creation.

Wilted Greens

Makes about 2 cups

> 1 tablespoon canola or other neutral oil
>
> 6 cups torn or whole sturdy greens,
>   stemmed if the stems are thick and fibrous
>
> ¼ teaspoon Diamond Crystal kosher salt
>   or ⅛ teaspoon other kosher salt

Heat a large sauté pan over medium-high heat. Add 1 ½ teaspoons of the oil. Swirl the pan to coat the bottom with oil, then add half of the greens. Sprinkle with half the salt. Stir or toss the greens in the pan. When wilted, remove from the pan and place in a bowl—grown-up spinach or baby kale take 10 seconds, cabbage or kale take a few minutes. Repeat the procedure with the remaining oil, greens and salt and then use when desired in your salad

Chiffonade Greens

This slicing technique bruises leaves less than chopping, and looks elegant.

Whole leaves, stemmed

Stack a few leaves and roll them lengthwise like a cigar. Use a sharp knife to slice the roll across into ribbons—slice very thin to use as a garnish, or wider for salad. If for some reason you are not using these chiffonade leaves immediately, you can wrap them loosely in paper towels, pop the package into a resealable plastic bag, and refrigerate for up to 3 days.

GRAINS AND RICE..

Noreen's Oat Groats

Noreen and Lee Thomas run the amazing Doubting Thomas Farms, about ten miles northeast of Fargo. While they primarily grow certified organic grains, soybeans, and oats, Noreen and her family always have side projects going: a high tunnel for growing heirloom seed plants; a mushroom house; egg chickens; bees; Icelandic lambs, and usually a few little piggies. We learned to just say yes when Noreen brought us products—it was always in our best interest.

Make 2 cups

1 cup raw oat groats*

½ teaspoon Diamond Crystal kosher salt
    or ¼ teaspoon other kosher salt

Oat groats are the oat kernels before the steel cutting or rolling for traditional oatmeals. Their texture is similar to barley or farro.

Soaking is optional but will reduce cooking time the following day. (It is purported to help break down starches in the oats so that the nutrients are more readily available.) Combine the raw groats with 3 cups water in a covered container. Let soak overnight.

recipe continues

Noreen Thomas snuggling her admittedly lovely crops at Doubting Thomas Farms.

Drain and rinse with fresh water. Add the groats, 1½ cups water, and the salt to a saucepan. Bring to a simmer over medium heat. Reduce the heat to medium-low, cover, and simmer for 20 to 30 minutes. The groats will increase in size and absorb most of the water when they are cooked through but still toothsome (not mushy). Drain if necessary, and transfer to a storage container. Let cool to room temperature, then cover. Refrigerate for up to 4 days.

Wild Rice

Wild rice is produced in the Upper Midwest in two forms: cultivated "wild" rice and authentically *wild* wild rice. The cultivated variety is cheaper. Authentic wild rice is a truly wild aquatic grass that is hand-harvested by whacking the seed pods into a canoe, and then sorting and drying the grains by hand. It is a very labor–intensive process that yields a slightly smoky grain of varying colors, from light green to dark brown. Real wild rice is a more delicate and special choice, but I have enjoyed cultivated wild rice my entire life. You can use them interchangeably—the choice is yours.

Makes 2 cups

> ½ cup wild rice, rinsed and drained
>
> ½ teaspoon Diamond Crystal kosher salt
>   or ¼ teaspoon other kosher salt

Combine the wild rice, salt, and 2 cups water in a 1-quart saucepan. Bring to a simmer over medium heat. Reduce the heat to low, cover, and continue at a low simmer until it has expanded but not popped—about 20 minutes for authentic wild rice and 40 to 50 minutes for cultivated. Remove from the heat and drain if necessary. Place in a covered container and chill. It will keep for up to 4 days.

Bulgur and Couscous

Both of these are staples of Sephardic (meaning the Jewish diaspora of Spain and North Africa) and Middle Eastern cuisine. They are easy to cook to boot.

Bulgur

Bulgur is cracked wheat that has been partially cooked, then dried. There are different sizes: fine, coarse, and very coarse. For a tabbouleh salad (page 230), a fine bulgur is traditional, but I like a coarse one because it adds texture.

Makes 2 cups

> 1 cup bulgur, rinsed
>
> ½ teaspoon Diamond Crystal kosher salt
>   or ¼ teaspoon other kosher salt

Combine the bulgur, 2 cups water, and the salt in a small saucepan. Bring to a boil over medium-high heat. Reduce the heat to low, cover and cook for 15 minutes or until most of the water has been absorbed. Remove from heat and drain if necessary. Let cool, then store in a covered container in the refrigerator for up to 4 days.

Couscous

Couscous is actually a pasta made from tiny balls of semolina that have been partially cooked and dried. Don't confuse it with Israeli (aka pearl) couscous, which you cook just like normal pasta.

Makes about 2 cups

> ½ teaspoon Diamond Crystal kosher salt
>   or ¼ teaspoon other kosher salt
>
> 1 cup couscous

Bring 1 cup water and the salt to a boil in a small saucepan. Stir in the couscous, remove from heat and cover. Let sit for about 10 minutes; all the water should be absorbed and the couscous should no longer be crunchy. If it is, keep it covered for a few more minutes

Fluff with a fork to separate the grains and pour onto a plate or baking sheet. If the couscous is clumping at all, continue to use the fork to break them apart. To store, cool to room temperature, cover container, and refrigerate for up to three days.

Hard–Boiled Eggs

The biggest challenge with hard–cooking farm–fresh eggs is to get them to peel smoothly without leaving the egg pockmarked and sad. If you aren't using farm–fresh eggs, 11–Minute Eggs will be easier. If you are, steaming is the way to go (see 20–Minute Eggs below).

To use the eggs in a salad, you can slice, halve, quarter, or shred them.

11–Minute Eggs (for Grocery Store Eggs)

Makes 6 eggs

> 1 tablespoon kosher salt (any brand)
> 6 large eggs

Prepare a large bowl of ice and water.

Bring about 1 inch of water to a boil in a large saucepan and add the salt. Add the eggs gently—they can crack if they hit the bottom of the pan too harshly—and reduce the heat to a simmer. Cover the pot and set a timer for 11 minutes.

When the timer rings, drain the eggs and place them in the ice water. Let cool until cold. Drain and peel. Store the peeled eggs in a covered container in the refrigerator for up to 4 days.

I like to peel hard-boiled eggs with my hands under cold running water—there is no scientific reason for this that I know of, but it always seems to work better.

20–Minute Eggs (for Fresh Eggs)

You need a steamer basket or something approximating one. The water that creates the steam shouldn't touch the eggs, so if you don't have a steamer basket, use a colander that fits inside the pot and lifts the eggs above the water.

Makes 6 eggs

6 large eggs

Prepare a large bowl of ice and water.

Add about 2 inches of water to a soup pot or large saucepan, place a steamer basket or colander inside, and cover. Bring to a boil over high heat, then reduce the heat to keep the water at a brisk simmer. Carefully add the eggs. Set a timer for 20 minutes.

When the timer rings, drain, chill, peel, and store the eggs as above.

Poached Eggs

Poached eggs are oh–so–photogenic and add a little French country elegance to a salad.

Makes 1 egg

1 teaspoon vinegar*
1 large egg, broken into a small cup

Use whichever kind is handy; a light-colored one won't stain the egg.

Bring 3 cups of water to a simmer in a medium saucepan. Reduce the heat to maintain a simmer and add the vinegar. Swirl the water with a spoon to create a small whirlpool (this helps the egg stay shapely), and gently pour the egg into the center of the vortex. Keep stirring the outskirts for about 30 seconds as the egg coagulates into a nice shape. Cook for 4 to 5 minutes more, until the white is set. Remove the egg with a slotted spoon and drain it briefly on a clean kitchen towel or paper towel before placing it on a salad. If not serving immediately, place it in a paper towel-lined container, cover, and refrigerate for up to 24 hours.

To make additional eggs, cook them one at a time. Once you are proficient with swirling the water, you can use a larger saucepan and poach multiple eggs at the same time.

Bacon Lardons

Bacon lardons are just Frenchified bacon bits.

Makes about ½ cup lardons, plus 1 to 2 tablespoons bacon fat

4 pieces bacon, preferably thick-cut

Stack the 4 pieces of bacon and cut it in half vertically so that you have 2 strips of equal length and about a ½ inch wide. Slice across the pieces of bacon at ½-inch intervals, giving you ¾ cup of raw pieces. Heat a saucepan over medium heat and add the bacon. Cook for 10 to 12 minutes, until some of the pieces are reddish-brown and cooked. Reduce heat to low and cook an additional 15 to 20 minutes, until they are to your liking—I like them crisp but still meaty. Remove with a slotted spoon and drain on paper towels, then sprinkle over a salad. Pour the fat into a jar to use later (if you like), or dispose of it in the trash (not down the drain!). If not using the lardons immediately, store them in a covered container in the refrigerator for up to 4 days. Warm them before using.

CRUNCH..

Toasted Nuts

You can toast any nut (or seed) to bring out different flavors.

Makes ½ to 1 cup

½ to 1 cup nuts of your choice*

If the nuts are large, you may want to chop them up.

Preheat the oven to 350°F. Spread the nuts on a baking sheet. Toast on the middle rack of the oven for 5 to 8 minutes, until they slightly darken. (Thinner or smaller nuts will toast more quickly so keep an eye on them.) Remove from the oven and let cool. If not using them immediately, store in a resealable plastic bag or covered container at room temperature for up to a week.

Spiced Nuts

Makes 1 cup

> ½ teaspoon Diamond Crystal kosher salt or other kosher salt
>
> 4 teaspoons granulated or brown sugar
>
> ½ teaspoon single or mixed spice*
>
> 1½ teaspoons oil or melted butter (any oil will do)
>
> 1 cup nuts of your choice, coarsely chopped if large (optional)

> *Some of my favorite spices are za'atar and ground sumac; dried chile mixes (especially with urfa biber and Aleppo pepper); minced fresh rosemary and chile flakes; herbes de Provence.*

Preheat the oven to 350°F. Combine the salt, sugar, spices, and oil or butter in a medium bowl.

Spread the nuts in one layer on a baking sheet. Toast until slightly darkened and fragrant, 5 to 9 minutes depending on size. Remove from the oven and add to the spice mixture. Toss to coat all the nuts. Pour back onto the baking sheet to cool. Once cooled, store in a resealable plastic bag or covered container at room temperature for up to a few weeks.

Candied Nuts

Tossing slightly salted nuts with an egg white whipped with sugar gives the nuts a real candy coating.

Makes 1 cup

> 1 large egg white
>
> 2 tablespoons granulated or packed brown sugar
>
> ½ teaspoon Diamond Crystal kosher salt or other kosher salt

recipe and ingredients continue

½ teaspoon spices (optional)*

1 cup nuts of your choice, coarsely chopped if large (optional)

Some of our favorite spices are za'atar and ground sumac; dried chile mixes (especially with urfa biber and Aleppo pepper); minced fresh rosemary and chile flakes; herbes de Provence.

Preheat the oven to 325°F. Line a baking sheet with parchment paper.

Whisk the egg white and sugar together until frothy. Whisk in the salt and spices (if using). Add the nuts and mix with a spatula or your hand (my preferred instrument) until thoroughly coated.

Spread the coated nuts on the prepared baking sheet. Toast in the oven for 12 to 15 minutes, stirring every 4 minutes to maintain even cooking, until slightly darkened and the coating looks dry. Remove from oven and let cool.

Store in a resealable plastic bag or covered container at room temperature for up to a few weeks.

Savory Granola

Makes 2 cups

1 cup rolled oats

½ cup sunflower seeds

½ cup flax or chia seeds

2 tablespoons canola oil

2 tablespoons honey, maple syrup, or agave syrup, or sugar in a pinch

1½ teaspoons Diamond Crystal kosher salt or ¾ teaspoon other kosher salt

2 teaspoons ground spices of your choice

Preheat the oven to 350°F. Line a baking sheet with parchment paper or foil.

Combine the oats, sunflower and flax (or chia) seeds, oil, honey, salt, and spices in a bowl until well mixed. Use your hands to clump the mixture together (to create crunchy clusters when baked) and then pour onto the prepared baking sheet. Toast on the middle rack in the oven for 8 minutes, until toasted and fragrant.

Reduce the heat to 300°F and toast for an additional 5 to 10 minutes. Every 4 minutes or so, stir the granola so the center gets as crunchy as the edges. Remove and cool on the baking sheet on a wire cooling rack. Store in a resealable plastic bag or covered container at room temperature for up to a few weeks.

Croutons

I like the cragginess of a torn crouton, but if your salad begs for a less rustic presentation, you can dice your bread. I prefer a fresh crouton with toasty edges and some chewiness to the center, but you can toast these longer to completely dry them out, which allows for longer storage.

We used day-old Focaccia or pita—both stale quickly and are easy to tear.

Makes about 2 cups or 1 ½ cups toasted breadcrumbs

2 cups torn or diced bread, crusts on*

¼ teaspoon Diamond Crystal kosher salt
or ⅛ teaspoon other kosher salt

2 teaspoons minced fresh parsley or ⅛ teaspoon dried

⅛ teaspoon chile flakes

1 small clove garlic, peeled and minced

1½ tablespoons oil**

Most choices of bread will work.
**I generally use olive oil, but melted butter, canola oil, or vegetable oil work, too.*

Preheat the oven to 350°F.

Combine the bread, salt, parsley, chile flakes, and garlic in a medium bowl. Pour the oil over, and work the oil and seasonings into the bread with your gloved hands.

recipe continues

Spread in a single layer on a baking sheet. Toast in the oven for 7 to 12 minutes, until the edges are darkened and they are at your preferred crunch level, depending on the size of the croutons—larger pieces require more time. Every 3 or 4 minutes, stir the croutons so that all pieces are evenly toasted. Let cool to room temperature and store in a resealable plastic bag for up to 2 days or freeze for up to a month. If they are chewy, and not completely dry, they may need to be refreshed in a 350°F oven for a few minutes and then cooled before adding to a salad.

TOASTED BREADCRUMBS: Even easier. Use 1½ cups freshly made breadcrumbs (whizzing bread in a food processor or blender works great), ¼ to ½ teaspoon kosher salt and 3 tablespoons oil. Toast in the oven for 8 to 12 minutes, stirring every so often to maintain even cooking. Watch more closely as the smaller pieces will cook more quickly. These will completely dry out, so will last at least a week at room temperature in a resealable plastic bag or covered container.

"LA PIÈCE DE RÉSISTANCE (DRESSING)...............................

French Camp Vinaigrette

In middle school, I went to French camp, part of the local Concordia Language Villages. My counselor, a hip Parisian named Nadège, made vinaigrette at the table—à la minute. It blew my teenage mind. I still make it today.

Makes about ¾ cup, enough for 4 largish salads

    1 tablespoon Dijon mustard*

    ¼ cup wine vinegar**

    ½ cup light olive or canola oil

    2 pinches of kosher salt

    1 turn of a pepper mill

*We used Grey Poupon at camp, but feel free to use any Dijon-style mustard, whole grain or smooth.

**Use red, white, sherry, or champagne—whichever you prefer.

Place the mustard and vinegar in a small bowl. Whisk together, and continue to whisk while slowly pouring in the oil. Season with the salt and pepper. Pour into a jar or bottle, cover, and store in the refrigerator for up to 2 weeks. (You may have to whisk or shake it before using after it has been chilled.)

If I have a teaspoon or so of mustard left in a jar, I add all the other ingredients, screw on the lid, and shake. It's a lazier version, if that's possible.

Standard Vinaigrette

Conventional wisdom suggests that the perfect oil–to–vinegar (or other acid) ratio is 3 to 1. That isn't tart enough for my palate—I prefer a range of 2.5 to 1—so I offer you my basic vinaigrette, which can withstand all sorts of substitutions (see below). Some vinegars or acidic components, like citrus juices, are more or less sour than others, so this is a recipe that you will want to taste as you substitute.

Vinaigrette lasts for a long time in a covered glass jar or bottle in the fridge. so feel free to scale up the batch. The oil might thicken from the cold, so let the vinaigrette warm up a bit before using. Also, you might need to shake or whisk it again to re-emulsify.

Makes 1 cup, more than enough for 4 entree salads

2 teaspoons Dijon mustard* (optional)

½ shallot, peeled and minced

⅓ cup wine vinegar**

¾ cup light olive, grapeseed, vegetable, or canola oil

2 pinches of kosher salt or sea salt (fine or coarse, your choice)

1 turn of a pepper mill

**Mustard helps to emulsify the dressing, and provides extra zing*
***Use red, white, sherry or champagne—whichever you prefer.*

recipe continues

Place the mustard, shallot, and vinegar in a bowl and whisk together. Continue whisking while slowly streaming in the oil. Season with the salt and pepper. Store in the refrigerator in a sealed bottle or closed container.

Here are some easy modifications:
- — Substitute mayonnaise for the Dijon mustard.
- — Add 1 teaspoon maple syrup, honey, or sugar to sweeten.
- — Whisk an egg yolk into the Dijon mustard first for a creamier dressing.
- — Add 1 peeled, minced garlic clove, or about ½ teaspoon grated fresh ginger root.
- — Add about 1 tablespoon minced fresh tender herbs (such as parsley, chives, or tarragon).
- — Substitute extra virgin olive oil for some of the oil.

Some of my other faves:
- — Red wine vinegar, fresh orange juice, fresh oregano, and olive oil
- — Yellow miso, rice vinegar, canola oil, and minced or pureed cucumber peel
- — Sherry vinegar, maple syrup, a splash of walnut oil, and canola or grapeseed oil

Ladolemono

We used this simple Greek lemon and olive oil mix to finish Hummus, toss with baby kale to place on top of an Egg Bake, and dress vegetables—its uses are endless.

Makes 1 cup, enough for 4 to 8 uses

Grated zest of 1 lemon (optional; adds a floral note)

½ cup fresh lemon juice (2½ to 3 lemons)*

½ cup extra virgin olive oil

*I prefer organic, thinner-skinned lemons, but any will do.

Put the lemon zest (if using), lemon juice, and olive oil in a bowl and whisk to combine. Or put them in a squeeze bottle, cap tightly, and shake the bottle to combine. Keep in the refrigerator for up to a month, to use whenever the urge strikes.

Russian Dressing

Equally usable on sandwiches, this is a tangy, slightly sweet, and vibrant throwback to salads of my childhood. Hello, iceberg!

Makes 1 cup, enough for 4 wedge salads or 6 sandwiches

1 scallion (green and white parts), root end trimmed, minced

1 tablespoon tomato paste

½ teaspoon Hungarian paprika

½ teaspoon urfa biber flakes

Pinch of freshly ground black pepper

½ teaspoon Diamond Crystal kosher salt
  or ¼ teaspoon other kosher salt

recipe and ingredients continue

Leaves from 1 sprig fresh thyme or oregano

Splash of hot sauce*

2 tablespoons red wine vinegar

2 tablespoons fresh lemon juice (about 1 lemon)

1 pickled Israeli pepper** or pickled mild banana pepper,
   drained and chopped

1 tablespoon brine from pickled peppers

Pinch of xanthan gum

½ cup canola oil

*I like Cholula.

**Pickled Israeli peppers are generally shipka peppers, slightly spicy
  and pickled in a sour brine. I find them at markets with Middle Eastern
  ingredients.

Place the scallion, tomato paste, paprika, urfa biber, black pepper, salt, thyme, hot sauce, vinegar, lemon juice, pickled pepper and brine, and xanthan gum in a blender jar, leaving the center of the lid open. Slowly drizzle in the oil while blending until you have an emulsified dressing. Store in the refrigerator for up to 2 weeks.

Celery–Cider Vinaigrette

I like this for its pronounced celery flavor—an acquired taste for some. It is sweet without being cloying, perfect for slaw. This can be easily made with a stick blender, jar blender, or by hand with a whisk.

Makes 1 cup, enough for 4 to 6 servings slaw

½ shallot, peeled and minced

1 tablespoon chopped fennel fronds

⅛ teaspoon celery seeds

1 teaspoon chopped fresh celery leaves

1 tablespoon chopped fresh parsley

¼ cup apple cider vinegar

1 tablespoon granulated sugar

½ teaspoon Diamond Crystal kosher salt
  or ¼ teaspoon other kosher salt

Pinch of xanthan gum

Pinch of freshly ground black pepper

⅔ cup canola oil

Put the shallot, fennel fronds, celery seeds and leaves, parsley, vinegar, sugar, salt, xanthan gum, and pepper in your blending container of choice. While blending or whisking continuously, drizzle in the oil. It should emulsify and mix into a thick dressing. Store in the refrigerator for up to 2 weeks.

Buttermilk–Poppy Seed Dressing

Old fashioned and delicious. I love this on fresh garden cucumbers with a touch of shaved red onion.

Makes 1 cup

½ cup buttermilk

1 tablespoon apple cider vinegar

1 tablespoon poppy seeds

½ shallot, peeled and minced

2 tablespoons mayonnaise

1 tablespoon honey

½ cup canola or grapeseed oil

Pinch of kosher salt (any brand)

2 turns of a pepper mill

Whisk together the buttermilk, vinegar, poppy seeds, shallot, mayonnaise, and honey in a bowl. While continuing to whisk, add the oil in a thin stream, until emulsified. Season with the salt and pepper. Store in the refrigerator for up to a week.

Sumac Vinaigrette

We used this dressing for our Fattoush Salad, a toasted bread salad with fresh cucumber, peppers, shaved fennel, orange supremes, and sumac-pickled onions.
The sumac and mint add distinctly Levantine flavors to a simple vinaigrette.

Makes about 1½ cups, enough for 4 or 5 large salads

>   2 tablespoons ground sumac*
>
>   1 tablespoon warm water
>
>   3 to 4 tablespoons fresh lemon juice (1 to 1 ½ lemons)
>
>   4 teaspoons pomegranate molasses**
>
>   2 cloves garlic, peeled and minced
>
>   ½ teaspoon Diamond Crystal kosher salt or ¼ teaspoon other kosher salt
>
>   1 tablespoon white wine vinegar
>
>   1 tablespoon minced fresh mint leaves or ½ teaspoon dried mint, crumbled
>
>   Pinch of xanthan gum
>
>   1 cup neutral oil (such as canola, vegetable or light olive oil)

>   *Sumac is a Middle Eastern spice made of ground sumac berries. It adds tart flavor and a beautiful deep red to a dish. We found ours online or at a local international food market.*
>
>   **Ditto with finding pomegranate molasses—it is a sweet and sour condiment made by reducing pomegranate juice and spices to a glaze.*

Combine the sumac and warm water in a small bowl. Let sit for 15 minutes.

Add the lemon juice, pomegranate molasses, garlic, salt, vinegar, and mint and whisk or use a stick blender to combine. Gradually add the oil in a thin stream while blending. Season with more salt, lemon juice, pomegranate molasses, and/or vinegar, if desired. Store refrigerated for up to a week.

Yogurt Dressing

Creamy, tart yogurt is a great foil for greens and vegetables. This is a base to which you can add all sorts of herbs and spices—scallions, any tender herb, curry powder, or turmeric to name just a few.

Makes a little over 1 cup

> ½ cup organic Greek yogurt (preferably whole milk)
>
> 2 tablespoons fresh lemon juice
>
> 1 tablespoon pomegranate molasses*
>
> 1 small clove garlic, peeled and minced
>
> ⅓ cup extra virgin olive oil
>
> *Pomegranate molasses can be found in any grocery or market with Middle Eastern ingredients. It is a thick, sweet-sour condiment made by reducing pomegranate juice and spices. To replace the pomegranate molasses if you can't find it, combine ¼ cup balsamic vinegar and 1 teaspoon sugar in a small saucepan over medium-low heat and simmer until it is reduced to a syrup.*

Whisk the yogurt, lemon juice, pomegranate molasses, and garlic together in a small bowl. While continuing to whisk, pour in the oil in a thin stream to create an emulsified dressing. Store in the refrigerator for up to a week.

Blue Cheese Dressing

I like this version for its simplicity—and because it is based on one my dad makes.

Makes about 1 cup, enough for 4 large salads

> 2 tablespoons mayonnaise
>
> 1 teaspoon Dijon mustard
>
> ½ cup sour cream or plain yogurt
>
> 2 tablespoons white wine vinegar
>
> ½ cup crumbled blue cheese*
>
> Pinch of kosher salt (any brand)
>
> 3 or more turns of a pepper mill
>
> *Choose a cheese you like to eat on its own. I like most blue cheeses, but Stilton or Roquefort make a kick-ass dressing.*

Whisk the mayonnaise, mustard, sour cream, and vinegar together in a small bowl. Add the blue cheese and mix with a spatula. Season with the salt and pepper. Add up to 1 tablespoon water if the dressing is too thick. Refrigerate for up to a week.

While you can combine the preceding salad elements as you like, here are a couple of specific salads that we made at BernBaum's.

Apple–Cucumber Tabbouleh

We served a version of this tabbouleh on its own, tossed with baby greens, and as part of the Vegetarian Bagel Plate with Beet Hummus, Baba Ghanoush, and a bagel. It is a hearty vegan salad where you can change up the vegetables according to what is in season. Some good combos we tried: apple and roasted winter squash, and cucumber, citrus supremes, and pomegranate seeds.

Serves 4 as a side salad

> 1 apple, cored and diced ¼ inch (about ¾ cup)
>
> ⅓ English cucumber, or 1 standard garden cucumber, peeled, seeded, and diced ¼ inch (¾ cup)
>
> Grated zest and juice from 3 to 4 lemons
>
> ¾ cup fresh parsley leaves, washed, dried, and minced
>
> ¾ cup fresh dill sprigs (small tender stems), washed, dried, and minced
>
> ¾ cup fennel fronds or fresh mint leaves, washed, dried, and minced
>
> 1 scallion (green and white parts), root end trimmed, thinly sliced
>
> 1½ cups Oat Groats (page 212) or coarse Bulgur (page 214)
>
> 2 tablespoons extra virgin olive oil
>
> ¾ teaspoon Diamond Crystal kosher salt or ½ teaspoon other kosher salt
>
> ¼ teaspoon urfa biber or Aleppo pepper flakes
>
> 2 turns of a pepper mill

Combine the apple, cucumber, lemon zest, about three-quarters of the lemon juice, parsley, dill, fennel fronds, and scallion in a large bowl. Mix gently with your gloved hands or a large spoon. Add the oat groats, olive oil, salt, urfa biber, and pepper and mix to combine. Check the seasoning—you may need more salt, pepper, and/or more lemon juice, depending on how tart you like it. Serve immediately or refrigerate in a covered container. This should keep for up to 4 days.

Horseradish–Caraway Potato Salad

Potato salad is a staple of picnics and Sunday dinner for a reason. It's a perfect cold side dish in the summer and a filling complement to meat all year long.

Serves 4 to 6 as a side dish

> 1½ pounds medium red-skinned potatoes, scrubbed
>
> 3½ teaspoons Diamond Crystal kosher salt
>   or 1¾ teaspoons other kosher salt
>
> ⅓ cup mayonnaise
>
> 3 tablespoons sour cream
>
> 4 teaspoons brown mustard (such as Gulden's)
>
> 2 teaspoons prepared horseradish
>
> ⅓ cup chopped cornichons or baby dill pickles
>
> 4 teaspoons cornichon or pickle brine
>
> 3 large Hard-Boiled Eggs (page 216), peeled and
>   coarsely chopped (not too small)
>
> 3 tablespoons minced fresh herbs (parsley, dill,
>   fennel fronds, tarragon, chives, etc.)
>
> 1½ teaspoons toasted caraway seeds*
>
> 3 turns of a pepper mill

**Toast spices in a dry sauté pan over medium heat. Once fragrant, remove
from the heat and cool, usually 2 to 3 minutes, before using.*

Place the potatoes in a medium saucepan. Cover with cold water by at least an inch and add 2 teaspoons of the salt. Bring to a boil over medium-high heat and cook the potatoes until just fork-tender (but not falling-apart tender), about 10 to 20 minutes depending on the size of your potatoes. Drain the potatoes in a colander. Set aside to cool to room temperature.

Whisk together the mayo, sour cream, mustard, horseradish, pickles and brine, eggs, herbs, and caraway seeds in a large bowl.

Dice the potatoes into 1-inch cubes or small wedges. Add them to the bowl and season with the remaining salt and the pepper. Gently mix with your gloved hand or a large spoon until completely coated. Store in a covered container in the refrigerator for up to 4 days.

Sweets

These recipes are mainly BernBaum's stalwarts with a few family recipes thrown in that we did not make regularly at the restaurant but are a sentimental addition for Vestur-Íslendingur like me and my family. We had many skilled bakers at BernBaum's, and because the bagels were finished by the time we opened, that left plenty of time to make sweets, always an easy sell in the Midwest.

Chocolate Almond Meringues

When my sister Jessica was an editor at a big publisher, she supplied me with many wonderful cookbooks that I wouldn't have known about otherwise. One of those, Viana La Place's *Dessert and Sweet Snacks*, offered a cookie recipe that I have adapted and used for at least 15 years. They are naturally gluten–free and a wonderful combination of dark chocolate, bitter cacao nibs, and sweet meringue.

Makes 12 to 14 cookies

> 8 ounces (1⅔ cups) raw skin-on almonds
>
> 3 large egg whites
>
> 1 tablespoon distilled white vinegar
>
> ¼ teaspoon Diamond Crystal kosher salt
>   or ⅛ teaspoon other kosher salt
>
> 1 cup granulated sugar
>
> 1 teaspoon vanilla extract
>
> 1⅓ cups 70% chocolate discs or chopped chocolate
>
> 1 cup cacao nibs (optional, but they add a great bitter chocolate note)

Preheat the oven to 350°F. Place the almonds on a baking sheet and toast for 5 to 7 minutes, until fragrant and slightly darker. Remove from the oven and let cool. Reduce the oven heat to 225°F.

Chop the almonds by hand or by pulsing to break up coarsely in a food processor and set aside.

recipe continues

Combine the egg whites, vinegar, and salt in the bowl of a stand mixer or a large bowl. Fit the stand mixer with the whisk attachment or use a handheld mixer with the beater attachment to whisk the egg whites to soft peaks. Gradually add the sugar, beating on high speed to stiff, shiny peaks. Gently mix the vanilla into the meringue. Dab a smidge of the meringue on the four corners of each of two baking sheets, then place sheets of parchment paper atop the baking sheets. (This will secure the parchment to the pans.)

For soft peaks, when the whisk is lifted, the peak of whipped egg whites should gently fold over like the top of a soft-serve ice cream cone. For stiff peaks, the peak will not fold over when the whisk is lifted.

Gently fold the almonds, chocolate, and cacao nibs (if using) into the meringue. Using a 2-ounce scoop or a serving spoon, spoon mounds of meringue onto the prepared baking sheets, spacing them 2 to 3 inches apart. Bake until the cookies release easily release from the parchment, but are not colored at all, 45 to 60 minutes. Remove from the oven and let cool to room temperature. These last for at least a week in a covered container at room temperature.

Folding is a gentle way to incorporate or stir two mixtures together without deflating them or overmixing. Use a spatula to scrape under the contents of the bowl, then turn the spatula over the top of the other side of the mixture and gently cut down. Continue with this while rotating the bowl until the two mixtures are lightly blended.

Dad in his second career as BernBaum's unpaid prep cook and tireless booster.

Vegan Mocha Tahini Cookies

As we were always searching for vegan recipes, chefs Sarah Strong and Cassie Witte came up with this amazing cookie.

Watch these while baking, as they can dry out quickly without the animal fat. Also, there is no harm in eating the dough raw—in fact, it is really good eating with a spoon straight out of the bowl.

Makes roughly 15 largish cookies or 35 smaller ones

⅓ cup tahini (aka tehina—ground sesame paste)*

½ cup extra virgin olive oil

½ cup packed light brown sugar

½ cup granulated sugar

⅓ cup brewed coffee, room temperature

2 teaspoons vanilla extract

2¼ cups all-purpose flour

½ teaspoon ground cinnamon

½ teaspoon baking soda

½ teaspoon Diamond Crystal kosher salt
 or ¼ teaspoon other kosher salt

1 scant cup bittersweet chocolate chips or a
 5-ounce bittersweet bar,** hand chopped

2 teaspoons flaky sea salt (such as Maldon)

To measure flour accurately by volume, scoop the flour into the measuring cup and level across the top of the cup with a knife or other flat utensil.

**Make sure that you have stirred the tahini well and incorporated the bits at the bottom of the jar before using it.*

***We used 70% chocolate, but anything over 50% should work.*

Combine the tahini, olive oil, brown sugar, and granulated sugar in the bowl of a stand mixer fitted with the paddle attachment. Pour in the coffee and vanilla and mix well. (You can also do this by hand with a whisk or spatula, or with a handheld mixer.)

Sift the flour, cinnamon, baking soda, and kosher salt together. Add to the tahini mixture and mix on low speed until just combined. Add the chocolate chips and mix until they are uniformly distributed throughout the dough.

Cover the bowl and chill the dough in the fridge for a couple of hours until it is firm. To refrigerate for up to 3 days before baking, transfer the dough to a sealed container. You can also place the dough on a sheet of wax paper, roll it into a log 3 inches in diameter and freeze it for up to a month. If it's frozen, defrost it in the refrigerator before cutting and baking.

Preheat the oven to 350°F, or 325°F if you're using convection. Line two baking sheets with parchment paper.

To make large cookies, use a 2-ounce scoop or heaping tablespoon; for smaller, use a ¾-ounce scoop or heaping teaspoon. Scoop the dough onto the prepared baking sheets, spacing the scoops at least 2 inches apart. Flatten each scoop with the palm of your hand and sprinkle with a pinch of sea salt. (If you rolled the dough into a log, cut slices about ¾-inch thick, lay them on the baking sheets the same way, and sprinkle with the sea salt. No need to flatten the slices.) Place one baking sheet on the middle rack of the oven and the other on the upper rack. Rotate the baking sheets after about 4 minutes and switch them between the racks to ensure even baking. Start checking the cookies after 6 minutes; they might take anywhere from 8 to 12 minutes, depending on your oven. You want to take them out just as they are turning slightly brown at the edges, browned at the bottom, and soft at the center. Do not overbake, as they dry out quickly!

Transfer the cookies, still on the parchment, to wire cooling racks to cool to room temperature. Store at room temperature in a sealed container for up to 4 days.

Rugelach

Rugelach means something like "little twisties" or "little corners" in Yiddish. In Eastern Europe in the 1800s, rugelach were small crescent-shaped pastries made with a yeasted dough. In the immigration of Ashkenazi Jews to the eastern United States over the past 150 years, rugelach became a different pastry, one made with a rich, unleavened dough generally containing cream cheese (which seems very mid-twentieth-century to me). The beauty of this adaptation is that the dough is easy to make and roll out. It also helps the cookies keep for longer than a yeasted dough would.

You can't have a Jewish lunch counter and not serve rugelach. We were inspired by both Noah and Rae Bernamoff's *Mile End Cookbook* and Flo Braker's *Sweet Miniatures: The Art of Making Bite-Size Desserts*. We kept to a chocolate-hazelnut filling and a fig-walnut filling, but feel free to improvise—as long as the filling is spreadable and tasty, it will be great.

Cream Cheese Pastry

Makes 32 rugelach

> 2 cups all-purpose flour
>
> 1½ teaspoons Diamond Crystal kosher salt
>   or ¾ teaspoon other kosher salt
>
> ½ pound (2 sticks) unsalted butter, cold, cut into ½-inch cubes
>
> One 8-ounce package cream cheese, cut into 1-inch cubes
>
> 2 tablespoons sour cream

USING A FOOD PROCESSOR: This is very easy to make in a food processor. Pulse the flour and salt until mixed. Add the butter and continue pulsing until the texture is a very coarse meal with ¼-inch pieces of butter. Dot with the cream cheese and sour cream. Pulse until the ingredients start to come together but aren't fully blended. Do not overmix—you want bits of fat to help create flaky layers in the dough.

MIXING BY HAND: This is slightly less easy. Pour the flour and salt into a large bowl and whisk to mix. Add the butter and cut it into the flour with a pastry blender (a great tool to have) or fork. You want to make a mixture with the texture of very coarse meal. Add the cream cheese and sour cream, continuing to cut through and mix until it looks like the fats are well distributed in the flour, but not homogeneous—like a good pie dough.

Dump the dough onto a clean counter and knead a few times to get it to come together. Divide in half, shape each portion into a circle, and flatten each with your palm to make it 1 to 2 inches thick. Cover each in plastic wrap and let sit for at least 30 minutes before rolling out. If you are making the dough ahead of time, it can be refrigerated for up to 2 days.

Fig–Walnut Filling

Makes 1½ cups, enough for at least 32 rugelach

> 1½ cups walnuts
>
> ¾ cup granulated sugar
>
> 1½ teaspoons ground cinnamon
>
> ¾ cup fig jam*

**We usually used Divina brand fig spread.*

Preheat the oven to 350°F. Spread the walnuts on a baking sheet and place on the middle rack of the oven. Toast until golden, 5 to 7 minutes. Remove from the oven and let cool.

USING A FOOD PROCESSOR: This is the easiest way. Place the walnuts in the work bowl with the sugar and cinnamon. Process until finely ground. Add the fig jam and pulse until it has fully mixed with the nuts and creates a large ball rolling around the work bowl.

MAKING BY HAND: Chop the nuts and sugar together by hand on a cutting board. Or place them in a heavy-duty resealable plastic bag, seal the bag, and bang on them with a small heavy skillet or mallet, until they look ground. Pour into a bowl and add the cinnamon and fig jam. Stir with a wooden spoon until well combined.

If not using immediately, refrigerate the filling in a covered container for up to a week or freeze for up to a month. Let it come to room temperature before trying to spread it on the dough. You may want to warm it in the microwave (just 20 to 30 seconds) to make it more spreadable.

Chocolate–Hazelnut Filling

This will be a gritty but spreadable paste, easier to work with than the fig version.

Makes about 2½ cups, enough for 48 rugelach

- ½ cup raw hazelnuts
- 3 tablespoons all-purpose flour
- 6 tablespoons granulated sugar
- 1 cup and 2 tablespoons bittersweet chocolate chips
- 6 tablespoons unsalted butter, cut into chunks, room temperature

Preheat the oven to 375°F. Place the hazelnuts on a baking sheet and toast until darker but not burnt, 5 to 7 minutes. Remove from the oven and let cool.

If you do not want nut skins in the filling, while the hazelnuts are still hot, pour them onto a clean kitchen towel and rub together to remove most of the skins.

Pulse the hazelnuts, flour, and sugar in a food processor until the consistency of sand. Add the chocolate and pulse to grind it into the nuts until fully incorporated. Add the butter in chunks and process until the filling is fully mixed and forms a large ball that rolls around the bowl. Use immediately. Or store in a covered container in the refrigerator for up to 2 weeks or in the freezer for up to a month. Bring to room temperature before using.

recipe continues

Finishing the Rugelach

Nonstick baking spray or unsalted butter, room temperature,
  for the pans

All-purpose flour, for dusting

1 batch Cream Cheese Pastry (page 246)

1 large egg

½ batch Fig-Walnut Filling (page 244)

⅓ batch Chocolate-Hazelnut Filling (page 245)

2 tablespoons turbinado sugar

Preheat the oven to 375°F. Line two baking sheets with parchment paper, then lightly spray or butter the parchment. (This is especially important if you're using the fig filling, as it sticks when it bakes.)

On a lightly floured work surface, roll out one round of dough to about ⅛ inch thick. Using a large pot lid or platter as a guide, cut a circle about 16 inches in diameter with a pizza cutter or chef knife. (At the restaurant, we placed a large stock pot lid on top of the dough and cut around it.) Set the dough circle aside on a piece of parchment paper or a lightly floured baking sheet. Repeat with the second round of dough. Lightly reflour the work surface and place the dough circles on it, a few inches from each other.

Make an egg wash by whisking the egg with 1 tablespoon water in a small bowl. With a pastry brush, brush the egg wash on the dough circles, leaving an outer ½-inch border clean. Spread a thin and even layer of filling on each dough circle to cover the egg wash, still leaving the border at the outer edge. (An offset spatula is the best tool for the job, although a knife, straight spatula, or your gloved hand can do the job.)

Use the pizza cutter to cut one circle evenly in half, then cut perpendicularly to the first cut, making four equal quarters. Bisect each of the quarters to get 8 wedges, then bisect those wedges, giving you 16 long, thin, equal-size wedges ❶. Wipe off the cutter as needed between cuts to keep it from sticking to the dough. Repeat with the other circle.

With each wedge of dough, pull it away from the rest and roll from the outside toward the pointy end ❷. Once rolled, place it on a prepared baking sheet and curl the ends toward you to make it more crescent-shaped. Space the rugelach 1½ to 2 inches apart. You can get 16 pieces easily on one 12 × 18-inch baking sheet.

Brush the rugelach with egg wash and sprinkle each with a good amount of turbinado sugar. Place one baking sheet on the middle rack of the oven and the other on the upper rack and bake for 8 to 12 minutes total, until golden brown. Rotate and switch the baking sheets halfway through (after about 4 minutes) to ensure even baking. Remove from the oven and let cool to room temperature. The rugelach keep for up to 4 days in a sealed container. They can be frozen at this point, but it is better to freeze unbaked.

> *Rugelach freeze incredibly well from an uncooked state; we froze them directly on the baking sheets, covered with a double layer of plastic wrap, for up to 2 weeks. Once frozen, you can throw them into a heavy duty resealable bag and keep in the freezer for up to 2 weeks. Defrost in the refrigerator, and bake as described above.*

Barb Lamb's Orange Rolls

Life in Fargo would be bland without friends like Peter Kelly and John Lamb, two dear people who happen to be second cousins. In 2010, Peter was my partner at Green Market, and gave me this family recipe to perk up our Saturday brunch. When I opened Bernbaum's, I made a few dozen even though they weren't technically on the menu. I figured this addictive, citrus–tinged sweet roll would remedy any opening week glitches. They were so popular, we added them to our weekend menu and they always sold through by noon. They're Fargo's equivalent of a cronut and they're worth the hype.

Makes 12 rolls

Sweet Dough

> 1 cup milk
>
> 3 tablespoons unsalted butter*
>
> 1⅛ teaspoons active dry yeast (½ packet)
>
> 4½ teaspoons water, body temperature**
>
> ½ cup granulated sugar
>
> Up to 4 cups all-purpose flour (depending on the humidity)
>
> ½ teaspoon Diamond Crystal kosher salt
>   or ¼ teaspoon other kosher salt
>
> 3 large eggs

**If using salted butter, omit the salt.*
***95 to 100°F; you can't feel a temperature change when you stick your finger in it.*

MAKING THE SPONGE: Heat the milk in a small saucepan over low heat or in a bowl in the microwave until small bubbles form; do not let it boil. Set aside to cool. Melt the butter in another small saucepan or in the microwave; set aside to cool.

Whisk the yeast and water in a large bowl until the yeast is dissolved. In another bowl, whisk together the sugar, 1 cup of the flour, and the salt.

Add the milk and butter to the yeast. Whisk in the eggs. Continue to whisk while adding the flour mixture slowly, making sure that there are no bits of dry flour left. Cover the bowl with plastic wrap and let the sponge rise at room temperature for 1½ to 2 hours, until it has about doubled in size.

MAKING THE DOUGH: You can either use a stand mixer with the paddle attachment to mix the dough, or a bowl and wooden spoon to mix it by hand. To use a mixer, place the sponge in the mixer bowl with 2½ cups of the remaining flour and mix until a soft dough forms. By hand, stir the flour into the sponge and mix until a soft dough forms. Depending on humidity and air temperature, you may need to add a bit more flour to get the dough to hold together. It should remain a very malleable dough to be tender, so don't add more than an extra ½ cup flour. Cover the bowl with a clean flour sack towel or plastic wrap, and let rise at room temperature until it has doubled, 45 minutes to 1½ hours.

To make the dough easier to roll out, refrigerate it for an hour or so after it has risen. However, this is not necessary.

Orange Filling

> 2 teaspoons grated orange zest
>
> ½ cup granulated sugar
>
> 8 tablespoons (1 stick) unsalted butter, room temperature

Combine the orange zest, sugar, and butter in a medium bowl until well mixed. Cover and let sit at room temperature until needed.

recipe continues

Finishing the Rolls

All-purpose flour, for dusting

1 batch Sweet Dough (page 248)

1 batch Orange Filling (page 249)

Nonstick baking spray

4 tablespoons (½ stick) unsalted butter, melted

Liberally flour the work surface and turn out the dough onto it. Roll out the dough to a rectangle roughly 14 × 12 inches with the longer side at the top. With an offset or straight spatula (offset is the best tool for this), spread the filling evenly on the dough, leaving a clean 1-inch border of dough along the top ❶. (Cover all of the rest of the dough to the edges.)

Roll up the dough jelly roll–style from the bottom, stopping 1 inch before the top edge ❷. (It does not need to be a tight roll; tight rolls will make the center of the roll spring out while baking, which is not a cardinal offense, but a different look!) Use a sharp knife or bench scraper to cut the roll into 12 equal-size snails ❸.

To cut a long roll into 12 pieces, I start by cutting it in half, then each half in half, then each quarter into thirds. It is easier to cut a piece of dough in half or thirds rather than to freestyle 12 equal pieces by eye. You can always pull out a ruler, but I'm a bit too lazy for that.

Spray a 12-compartment muffin tin. To shape each roll to go into the pan, stretch the tail of the snail (the inch of dough without filling) under the spiral to catch the filling during baking. Place the roll in the pan with the tail on the bottom. Repeat with the rest of the snails.

If you will be baking soon, cover the pan loosely with plastic wrap and let rise at room temperature until the rolls puff over the top of the muffin tin, about 30 minutes. Alternately, if you want fresh morning rolls, wrap the pan in plastic and refrigerate until the next morning.

If the rolls have been in the refrigerator overnight, take them out, loosen the plastic wrap, and let them rise for 45 minutes to an hour.

While the shaped rolls are rising, preheat the oven to 375°F.

Unwrap the muffin tin and place it on a baking sheet to catch any spills. Place on the middle rack in the oven and bake for 12 to 15 minutes, rotating the muffin tin after about 6 minutes for even baking. I like them golden brown to brown, not pale yellow ❹. Remove from the oven and brush with melted butter. Let the rolls sit in the pan to cool so that they will hold their shape once removed. Serve immediately after cooling.

These freeze pretty well in a heavy-duty resealable plastic bag, for up to a month. But there is nothing like one fresh out of the oven.

Chocolate Babka Rolls

We made our chocolate babka rolls with the same dough as the orange rolls—just the filling and the shape differ. (Thanks to pastry chef Monica McCoy for realizing we could repurpose our sweet dough!)

To break this project into smaller parts, make the streusel and filling up to a week ahead and bring them to room temperature before using. You can make the dough, and give it a first rise, then refrigerate it the night before you bake.

Makes 12 rolls or two 8½ × 4½-inch loaves

Chocolate Babka Streusel

½ cup all-purpose flour

3 tablespoons granulated sugar

4½ teaspoons unsweetened cocoa powder

½ teaspoon Diamond Crystal kosher salt
  or ¼ teaspoon other kosher salt

4½ tablespoons (just over ½ stick) unsalted butter, cold,
  cut into ½-inch cubes

⅓ cup bittersweet chocolate chips

USING A FOOD PROCESSOR: This is easiest. Add the flour, sugar, cocoa, and salt to a food processor bowl. Pulse to mix completely. Add the butter and chocolate chips, then pulse until the mixture is the texture of coarse meal with some pea-sized lumps of butter and chocolate.

MIXING BY HAND: This works almost as well. Whisk the flour, sugar, cocoa, and salt together in a large bowl. Add the butter and cut it in with a pastry blender or a fork until the mixture is the texture of a coarse meal. Stir in the chocolate chips.

If not using immediately, place it in a covered container and store in the refrigerator for up to a week or the freezer for up to a month.

Chocolate Babka Filling

7 tablespoons unsalted butter, cut into chunks

½ cup bittersweet chocolate chips, or a 3-ounce bittersweet bar, hand chopped

¾ cup granulated sugar

2 tablespoons unsweetened cocoa powder

Melt the butter and bittersweet chocolate together in the top of a double boiler or in the microwave. To create a double boiler: Put the butter and chocolate in a heatproof bowl (preferably stainless steel) that is slightly wider than a medium saucepan. Fill the saucepan with 1 to 2 inches of water and bring the water to a simmer over medium-high heat. Place the bowl atop the saucepan, not touching the water. Reduce the heat to maintain a simmer. Stir the chocolate and butter while they melt. Once completely melted and mixed, remove the bowl from the saucepan and set aside to cool.

To use the microwave, place the butter and chocolate in a microwave-safe bowl. Microwave on high in 45-second increments, stirring between intervals, until it is completely melted and mixed. Set aside to cool.

It is important not to overheat chocolate when melting it, as it can burn.

Whisk the sugar and cocoa powder into the butter-chocolate mixture. If not using immediately, cover the bowl and refrigerate for up to a week, letting it come to room temperature before using.

recipe continues

Finishing the Chocolate Babka Rolls

All-purpose flour, for dusting

1 batch Sweet Dough (page 248), ready for rolling and shaping

1 batch Chocolate Babka Filling (page 253)

1 batch Chocolate Babka Streusel (page 252)

2 ounces bittersweet chocolate (chips or chopped)

4 tablespoons (½ stick) unsalted butter, melted

Line two baking sheets with parchment paper. Liberally flour the work surface and turn out the dough onto it. Roll the out dough out to a rectangle roughly 16 × 12 inches, with a longer side at the top. With an offset or straight spatula (offset is the best tool for this), spread the filling evenly on the dough, all the way to the edges. Sprinkle the streusel evenly over the filling ❶.

Fold in the right and left sides to meet in the center ❷.

Fold the right side over the left so the outside edges meet on the left. You should end up with a rectangle that is 4 × 12 inches ❸.

Folding the sides into the center, then folding one side over the other, is called a "book fold."

Cut the rectangle horizontally into 12 equal strips: first cut it in half, then cut each half in half, and finally each quarter into equal thirds ❹.

Flatten a strip, pulling it gently and twisting until it is about 6 to 8 inches long ❺, before making a single knot with it ❻. Place it on a prepared baking sheet.

Repeat with the rest of the strips, placing them at least 2 inches apart. (They may look like twisted blobs, but will be great once baked.)

Cover the baking sheets loosely with plastic wrap and let the rolls rise at room temperature until they are about 1½ times their original size, about 30 minutes. Alternately, if you want fresh morning rolls, you can wrap the pans tightly in plastic and refrigerate until the next morning.

If the rolls have been in the refrigerator overnight, take them out, loosen the plastic wrap, and let them rise for 45 minutes to an hour.

recipe continues

While the shaped rolls are rising, preheat the oven to 375°F. Melt the chocolate in a double boiler or the microwave (see page 253) and set aside.

Unwrap the baking sheets and place one on the middle rack and the other on an upper rack in the oven. Bake for 12 to 15 minutes, rotating and switching the pan after about 6 minutes for even baking. (I like these golden brown to brown.)

Remove from the oven and brush with the melted butter. After the rolls have cooled for a few minutes, drizzle with the melted chocolate. Serve immediately or later the same day.

These freeze pretty well in a heavy-duty resealable plastic bag, for up to a month. But there is nothing like one fresh out of the oven.

Chocolate Babka Loaf

This is a chocolate babka roll writ large, and the traditional way of making this Jewish classic. The basic difference is in the rolling and shaping. You can use two small loaf pans, or a baking sheet—whichever works for you in terms of shape.

> 3 tablespoons unsalted butter, melted, plus more for greasing the pans (optional)
>
> Nonstick baking spray (optional)
>
> All-purpose flour, for dusting
>
> 1 batch Sweet Dough (page 248), ready for rolling and shaping
>
> 1 batch Chocolate Babka Filling (page 253)
>
> 1 batch Chocolate Babka Streusel (page 252)
>
> 3 tablespoons melted bittersweet chocolate*
>
> *Melted in the microwave or double boiler; see page 253.*

Butter or spray two 8½ × 4½-inch loaf pans or a baking sheet. For easier clean up, line each with parchment paper. Lightly flour a work surface or board.

Roll out the dough on the work surface to a 12 × 16-inch rectangle, with the longer side at the top. Spread the filling evenly over the dough to the edges ❶. Sprinkle evenly with the streusel.

Roll the rectangle into a log from the bottom up, jelly-roll-style, not using too much or too little pressure ❷. Even pressure will make a good babka. Cut the log into two equal pieces.

recipe continues

Slit each log end to end through the middle, all of the way through, so that the inside layers of the log are visible ❸.

With 2 halves of a log, gently and loosely twist them together so that the uncut sides of the log halves are on the interior of the twist and the cut sides (showing the dough layers) are on the outside of the twist ❹.

Place each twisted log in a loaf pan or side by side on the baking sheet, about 4 inches apart. Cover loosely with plastic wrap and let rise at room temperature for 1½ to 2 hours, until they look nicely puffed. If you are using 3-inch deep loaf pans, they will rise to fill the pan three-quarters to the top when ready to bake.

While the loaves are rising, preheat the oven to 375°F.

Place the loaf pans or baking sheet on the middle rack of the oven and bake for 40 to 50 minutes, rotating the pan(s) after about 20 minutes to ensure even baking. If a loaf looks like it is getting too dark while baking, place foil loosely atop to cover. The babka will be done when a cake tester or skewer comes out clean of dough and an instant-read thermometer inserted in the center reads about 190°F.

Remove from the oven and place on a wire cooling rack or wooden board. Brush with the 3 tablespoons melted butter and let cool for 10 minutes. Drizzle with the melted chocolate. When the loaves have sat for an additional 30 minutes, they are ready to slice and serve.

To keep the babkas for a few days, place in a resealable plastic bag and leave at room temperature. You can freeze the loaves, well-wrapped, for up to a month, although nothing is quite as good as babka straight from the oven.

Bread Pudding

If by some bizarre circumstance you have leftover Orange or Babka Rolls (pages 248 and 252), or even Challah (page 29), this is a fantastic dessert. We liked to serve it oven–warmed, with Caramel Sauce (page 261), whipped Crème Fraîche (page 112), and Crumble (page 262).

Serves 6 to 8

> 6 tablespoons (¾ stick) butter, melted and cooled,
>   plus more for the pan (optional)
>
> Nonstick baking spray (optional)
>
> 4 Babka Rolls (page 252), Orange Rolls (page 248),
>   or 1-inch-thick slices Challah (page 29)
>
> 4 large eggs, beaten
>
> 1 cup milk
>
> 1½ cups heavy cream
>
> ½ cup granulated sugar
>
> 1½ teaspoons vanilla extract

Butter or spray the sides and bottom of a 10-inch square baking pan or 10-inch quiche or pie plate. Place parchment paper on the bottom.

Cut the rolls into cubes of about 1 inch and place in the prepared pan. Whisk together the eggs, milk, cream, melted butter, sugar, and vanilla in a large bowl. Pour over the cubes, making sure to coat them on all sides. Cover with plastic wrap and refrigerate for at least 1 hour or up to overnight.

Preheat the oven to 325°F. Remove the bread pudding from the refrigerator and replace the plastic wrap with foil.

Bake on the middle rack of the oven for 30 minutes or until just set. Take off the foil and bake an additional 10 minutes to brown the top. Let cool to room temperature, then cut into 6 to 8 pieces.

This keeps in the refrigerator, covered, for up to 6 days. Or tightly wrap in plastic and freeze for up to a month.

Caramel Sauce

A perfectly simple and tasty caramel sauce for all your caramel needs. If you haven't worked with molten sugar before, please be careful—it makes a nasty burn, something I know from experience. Before starting to cook the sugar, make sure that you have a pastry brush and cup of water at the ready, and the cream warmed. This is great on Bread Pudding (page 259) or anything else your heart desires.

Makes 1½ cups, enough for 6 servings

> 1 cup granulated sugar
>
> 4 teaspoons light corn syrup
>
> 1 cup heavy cream, warmed*
>
> *Warm for about 30 seconds on high in the microwave, or in a small saucepan over low heat on the stove.*

Pour 2 tablespoons water into a medium saucepan. Pour the sugar and corn syrup into the center of the pan. Heat over medium-high heat until actively bubbly. Reduce the heat to low to continue to cook at a low boil.

At this point, if you see opaque white crystals forming, use a pastry brush dipped in water to brush water around the inside walls of the pot. The tiny addition of water will help keep the sugar in solution (melted into the water), which is what you want.

As the sugar melts, the syrup will turn clear. Once the syrup starts to turn a light golden color, start paying closer attention to it.

The syrup will deepen in color to dark amber or medium brown. (It may feel like you are waiting too long before it darkens, but stay vigilant! It can change from golden to black and smoky really quickly.) Take the pot off the heat and pour the cream in slowly while stirring with a wooden spoon or heatproof spatula.

The caramel may solidify momentarily with the addition of the cream but will smooth out again as you stir. Once the sauce has slightly cooled, it is ready to use.

For later use, let cool to room temperature before pouring into a covered container and storing in the refrigerator. Caramel sauce can keep for a week or more in the refrigerator. To reheat, microwave for 30 seconds until pourable or warm gently on the stovetop.

Crumble

Another Monica McCoy invention. I love eating this by the handful as a snack, but it is great as a garnish on Bread Pudding (page 259), or sprinkled on ice cream, frozen yogurt or any other dessert crying out for a crunchy element.

Makes about 3 cups

> 1 cup almonds*
>
> 1 cup granulated sugar
>
> ½ cup all-purpose flour
>
> ½ cup flaked coconut (preferably unsweetened)
>
> Pinch of ground cinnamon
>
> 8 tablespoons (1 stick) butter**

> *You can use skin-on, roasted or raw, preferably unsalted. Feel free to substitute hazelnuts or walnuts for the almonds.*
>
> **If using unsalted butter, add a pinch of salt.*

Preheat the oven to 325°F. Line a baking sheet with parchment paper.

Pulse the almonds in a food processor until coarsely chopped. Transfer half of them to a medium bowl. Add the sugar to the food processor and process the remaining almonds to a sand-like consistency. (You can do this by hand, but it will take much more chopping to get the second half processed.) Add the almond-sugar mixture to the bowl. Whisk in the flour, coconut, and cinnamon.

Melt the butter in a saucepan or the microwave and pour it into the bowl. Mix with a spatula until everything is moistened. Crumble the mixture onto the prepared baking sheet. Bake for 5 to 7 minutes, until toasted. Remove from the oven and let cool.

Once cool, break the crumble into little clumps. To store for later use, place in a resealable plastic bag or covered container and store at room temperature for a week or more. This freezes well, too.

Noodle Kugel, Two Ways

A dish that mixes sweet and savory, kugel proved to be sometimes confusing to our customers. It was our entry into a local Hotdish Festival a few years back, prompting many tasters to call it "interesting." (In the Midwest, "interesting" can mean anything from unexpected to disgusting.) One judge, who happens to be Jewish, loved it. Since it is really just creamy noodles with a crunchy sweet topping, it is comfort food, and I believe the Midwest will come around to it.

I really enjoy the crunch of Grandma Bonnie's streusel, but have included a more traditional streusel recipe as well. This is a great side for a meaty main course like brisket. It's also good by itself as a hearty dinner casserole.

Serves 12 as a side dish and 8 as a main

Kugel

12 ounces egg noodles*

3 teaspoons Diamond Crystal kosher salt
  or 1½ teaspoons other kosher salt

1 cup sour cream

One 8-ounce package cream cheese, room temperature**

½ cup granulated sugar

4 large eggs

1 cup heavy cream

1 cup buttermilk

Unsalted butter, for greasing

*This is generally one package. If you have a 1-pound package,
 use three-quarters of it.*

**For a lighter custard, substitute 1 cup cottage cheese, blended
 until smooth.*

Fill a stock pot or large soup pot two-thirds full of water. Add 2 teaspoons of the salt and bring to a boil over high heat. Once boiling, add the egg noodles and reduce heat to maintain a boil, but not an overflowing mess. Cook until the noodles are almost fully cooked, but with a little bite to them, usually a minute or two less than the time given on the package. Drain the noodles in a colander in the sink and cool by running cold water over them.

recipe continues

Use a food processor or blender for the custard. Blend the sour cream, cream cheese (or cottage cheese), and granulated sugar to a smooth paste. Add the eggs and blend until well mixed. Add the cream, buttermilk, and the remaining salt and pulse to fully mix, but do not aerate the custard too much.

Butter a 9 × 13-inch baking pan. Spread the noodles evenly in the pan. Pour the custard over the noodles and let sit for 15 minutes so the noodles and custard can meld a bit. If not baking the kugel immediately, cover with plastic wrap and refrigerate for up to 3 days.

Grandma Bonnie's Streusel (optional)

> 2 cups corn flakes
>
> 4 tablespoons (½ stick) butter, melted
>
> 1 packed cup brown sugar
>
> ¼ teaspoon ground cinnamon

Put the corn flakes in a large bowl. Pour the butter over them and sprinkle the brown sugar evenly on top, along with the cinnamon. Gently combine with your gloved hands or a spatula.

Brett's Favorite Streusel (optional)

> 1 packed cup brown sugar
>
> 1 cup all-purpose flour
>
> ¼ teaspoon ground cinnamon
>
> ½ teaspoon Diamond Crystal kosher salt
>   or ¼ teaspoon other kosher salt
>
> 8 tablespoons (1 stick) unsalted butter, cold, cut into ½-inch cubes

Combine the brown sugar, flour, cinnamon, and salt in a bowl. Mix well before cutting in the butter with a pastry blender or fork. You want to create a coarse cornmeal texture.

Finishing the Kugel

1 batch Kugel

1 batch Streusel (your choice)

Preheat the oven to 350°F.

Uncover the baking pan, if necessary, and place on the middle rack in the oven. Bake for 20 minutes. Pull the pan out of the oven and spread your choice of streusel evenly over the top. Return to the oven and bake another 10 minutes or until the custard is just set (no longer liquid) and the streusel is nicely browned. Remove from the oven and let sit for 15 minutes before cutting into 8 to 12 pieces.

The baked kugel keeps, covered, in the refrigerator for up to 3 days. The easiest way to warm up leftovers is in the microwave on high for 2 to 3 minutes. You can also reheat in an oven safe pan at 350°F for 7 to 10 minutes until hot.

Grandma Effie and
Grandma Gladys
in 1970.

At left: Effie's shorthand
kleinur recipe.

Kleinur
2 c sugar
2 eggs
3 T Melted Butter
1⅛ c Milk
2 tsp BP
1 tsp Vanilla
1 tsp Salt
about 4⅓ C flour

Kleinur

Growing up, there were always kleinur (Icelandic doughnut twists) at Grandma Effie's house. They freeze well, so she would make a large batch and have some out—as well as a hundred other treat options—for snacking when we visited. I have made her recipe quite a few times, but mine never taste the same. They are good, but aren't infused with the same intense grandma love that Effie's were.

These cardamom-scented, crispy twists of dough have lots of surface area to coat with sugar. Serve them with strong coffee. My recent experience in Iceland proved that these are still a common bakery treat, although the Icelandic versions are supersized, very puffy, and without the defining cardamom flavor I'm accustomed to.

Makes 35–40 donuts

1 large egg

1 cup granulated sugar, plus 1 cup more for coating

1½ tablespoons unsalted butter, melted and cooled

¼ teaspoon vanilla extract

½ cup milk

1 teaspoon baking powder

½ teaspoon Diamond Crystal kosher salt
    or ¼ teaspoon other kosher salt

½ teaspoon ground cardamom

¼ teaspoon ground or freshly grated nutmeg

2½ cups all-purpose flour, plus more for dusting

Neutral oil, such as vegetable or canola, for frying

Whisk the egg in a large bowl, to break the yolk. Add the sugar, butter, vanilla, and milk and whisk to combine. In another bowl, whisk together the baking powder, salt, cardamom, nutmeg, and flour. Slowly stir the dry ingredients into the wet ones with a wooden spoon or sturdy spatula. Once the dough gets too stiff for stirring, knead it by hand until no dry patches remain. Divide the dough into two balls and wrap each in plastic. Refrigerate for at least an hour or up to overnight.

If you have a deep fryer, you are in luck. Fill it with oil and heat to 325°F according to the manufacturer's directions. Otherwise, pour at least 2 inches of oil into a heavy, wide-bottomed pot. (I use my grandma's very heavy and well-seasoned 4-inch-deep cast-iron skillet.) Heat the oil slowly over medium heat. You want it to

recipe continues

reach 325°F but not burn, so keep an eye on it while it is heating. If it is getting too hot, remove it from the burner, then bring it back to 325°F when you're ready to fry. Line one or two baking sheets with several layers of paper towels and set aside next to the deep-fryer or stove.

Generously flour a counter or board. Place one of the dough portions on the counter and roll it out to a rectangle about ⅛ inch thick. With a pizza wheel or sharp knife, cut the dough lengthwise into strips 1½ to 2 inches wide ❶.

Then cut the dough crosswise so that each strip is roughly 4 inches long. (The dough will resemble a grid.) Cut a lengthwise slit about 2 inches long in the center of each rectangle, being careful not to cut through to the end ❷.

You could twist the dough right now, but I find that the kleinur maintain their shape better if twisted right before I drop them into the oil.

Test that the oil is ready by frying an end strip of dough or a chunk of bread. If it sizzles and turns golden immediately, it's probably there. (To be positive, check with a deep-frying thermometer, if you have one.) Working with a few rectangles at a time, fold one short end through the slit to give you an elongated twist ❸ (almost a double helix) and drop it carefully into the oil ❹. Depending on the size of your pan or fryer, you can probably fry 5 or 6 kleinur at a time.

Maintaining the oil temperature in a pot is somewhat tricky—you may have to adjust heat every few minutes.

Fry the kleinur until they float, about 20 seconds. Turn them over with a slotted spoon or spider (my favorite tool for this) and fry until golden on the other side ❺. Remove from the oil and place on the prepared baking sheet. Continue frying additional batches until you have used all of the cut dough.

Repeat with the second half of the dough. You may want to turn off the heat under the oil while roll and cutting this batch so that it doesn't get too hot.

If serving them immediately, pour 1 cup of sugar into a large bowl or heavy paper bag. Dunk a few of the kleinur in the sugar and toss or shake to coat them. If not serving immediately, store them unsugared in a covered container or resealable plastic bag at room temperature for up to 4 days. They also freeze beautifully in a heavy-duty resealable plastic bag for up to a month. Defrost at room temperature. To get them crunchy again if they were stored or frozen, heat them on a baking sheet in a 350°F oven for 4 to 6 minutes, then toss in granulated sugar.

Amma Cindy's Pönnukökur

These Icelandic crêpes formed the base of our Blintzes—and worked better than a traditional crêpe, in my opinion.

My mother (aka Amma Cindy) combined her mother's and grandmother's recipes to come up with this perfect one. You can make these to fill and fry as Blintzes (page 272), but they are tremendous on their own with a bit of lingonberry jam and whipped Crème Fraîche (page 112) or Sweet Skyr (page 116) folded inside.

Makes 12 to 15 crêpes

> 2 large eggs
>
> 1¾ cups whole milk
>
> ½ cup heavy cream
>
> 1 teaspoon vanilla extract
>
> 2 tablespoons granulated sugar
>
> 1¼ cups all-purpose flour
>
> ¼ teaspoon baking powder
>
> ½ teaspoon ground cardamom
>
> ½ teaspoon ground or freshly grated nutmeg*
>
> 1 teaspoon Diamond Crystal kosher salt or ½ teaspoon other kosher salt
>
> Unsalted butter, for frying**
>
> *Freshly grated on a Microplane is preferable.*
> **I use a butter stick that is still half-wrapped; the wrapping makes a hand hold.*

In a large bowl, whisk the eggs to break the yolks. Whisk in the milk, cream, and vanilla, ensuring they are completely mixed in. You can also mix with a stick blender. Or combine everything in a blender jar, cover, and pulse until well blended.

Sift the sugar, flour, baking powder, cardamom, and nutmeg into another bowl. Whisk in the kosher salt.

MIXING BY HAND OR STICK BLENDER: Slowly pour the dry ingredients into the wet while whisking or blending.

MIXING IN A BLENDER: Add the dry ingredients to the blender jar and pulse to mix. Stop the blender and scrape down the sides of the jar so nothing dry remains.

Amma Cindy circa 1993, warm *and* chic in her Icelandic wool beret!

Cover and refrigerate the batter for at least an hour or up to 3 days ahead.

Heat your pan over medium-high heat. Spread a thin film of butter over the surface. (I hold a half-wrapped butter stick by the wrapper and swirl the end of the stick around the hot pan for exactly the right amount.) If the pan is hot enough, the butter will foam immediately. Ladle in ¼ cup batter (a 2-ounce scoop) while tipping the pan to create an evenly thin layer that reaches the rim of the pan. Cook until the batter looks set, 30 to 90 seconds, depending on the heat of the stove. Flip with a fish spatula. Cook the second side for 10 to 20 seconds. Both sides should have browned spots throughout. Remove and stack on a plate, separating the crêpes with wax paper. Rebutter the pan between crêpes and keep frying until you have used up all the batter.

A pönnukökur pan is a flat round pan with a shallow lip. You can get one at an Icelandic import store. If you don't have one, use a large crêpe pan or 10-inch nonstick skillet.

Serve immediately, plain or filled as suggested. Or let them cool and store at room temperature in a resealable plastic bag to use the same day to make Blintzes (page 272). I don't recommend refrigerating or freezing pönnukökur—they lose much of their considerable charm.

Blintzes

If you are using Pönnukökur (page 270) as the base, I recommend that you fill them before refrigerating; the crêpes become less pliable when refrigerated. You can serve these as a side or dessert for 6 or a meal for 4, albeit not too nutritionally balanced.

We served these with a dollop of lingonberry preserves, but any kind will work. Fresh fruit would be lovely, too.

Makes 2 cups filling and 12 to 15 blintzes

Blintz Filling

1 heaping cup cottage cheese

1¼ packages (10 ounces total) cream cheese,
    room temperature

⅓ cup granulated sugar

Grated zest of 1 lemon

1 large egg yolk

½ teaspoon vanilla extract

Mixing by machine: Blend the cottage cheese in a food processor or in a jar blender until smooth. Add the cream cheese, sugar, lemon zest, egg yolk, and vanilla and pulse until evenly mixed.

Mixing by hand: Press the cottage cheese through a sieve into a bowl, then stir in the cream cheese, sugar, lemon zest, egg yolk, and vanilla. Or most easily, just whisk all the ingredients together until they are completely mixed.

Use immediately or refrigerate in a covered container for up to 4 days. Do not freeze.

recipe continues

Blintzes

1 batch Pönnukökur (page 270), or 12 to 15 crêpes (10-inch diameter)

1 batch Blintz Filling (page 272)

8 tablespoons (1 stick) unsalted butter, cut into 4 chunks

1 cup lingonberry or other preserve (optional)

Powdered sugar, for serving (optional)

Place a pönnukökur on a clean counter or board. Spoon a large tablespoon of filling across the bottom center. Fold the bottom edge up and over the filling to spread it 3 inches across, leaving an inch or so at each side. Fold in each side over the filling, then roll it up from bottom to top—in other words, roll it like a burrito. Repeat with the remaining pönnukökur and filling. If not cooking and serving immediately, layer them, separated with wax paper, in a covered container and refrigerate for up to 4 days.

Heat a frying pan over medium heat. Add a chunk of butter—if the pan is the right heat, the butter will melt and foam almost immediately. Add up to 4 blintzes and fry until golden on the bottom, about 2 minutes. Use a fish spatula to turn them over, and fry the other side. Remove from heat and serve immediately, sprinkled lightly with powdered sugar or topped with preserves. To serve later, lay the fried blintzes on a baking sheet, cover lightly, and hold at room temperature for up to 30 minutes. Reheat uncovered in the oven at 350°F for 3 to 5 minutes, until heated through.

Vínarterta

Meaning "Viennese torte" in Icelandic, this is another classic recipe from my grandmother's kitchen. It tastes like a Fig Newton gone wild—seven layers of cookie sandwiched with fruit filling. My grandma went for the traditional prune lightened with a bit of apricot, but you can use any jam or preserve. (You'll need about 7 cups.) This is a pretty and impressive dessert, perfect as part of a dessert or cookie assortment.

You'll need multiple baking sheets to make this efficiently. If you only have one or two, each time you remove them from the oven, slide the parchment with the baked dough on to the cooling rack, line the baking sheet with fresh parchment paper, and set another sheet of dough on it to return to the oven. You should take care not to burn yourself, but the pans themselves do not need to be cooled between batches.

Since one vínarterta makes a large batch, you can also halve it and double wrap in plastic before freezing one or both portions for up to a month.

Makes about forty 1 × 2½-inch pieces

1 teaspoon baking soda

1 teaspoon baking powder

3 teaspoons ground cardamom

6 cups all-purpose flour, plus more for dusting

½ pound (2 sticks) unsalted butter, room temperature

2½ cups granulated sugar

4 large eggs

½ cup sour cream

1 teaspoon vanilla extract

1½ pounds pitted prunes (about 3½ cups)

18 ounces dried apricots (about 3 cups)

To measure flour accurately by volume, scoop the flour into the measuring cup and level with a knife or other flat utensil.

Whisk together the baking soda, baking powder, 2 teaspoons of the cardamom, and the flour in a large bowl. Place the butter and 2 cups of the sugar in the bowl of a stand mixer, fit the mixer with the paddle attachment, and cream the butter and sugar on medium speed until light, 3 to 5 minutes. Add the eggs one at a time, adding another only after the previous one has been mixed in. Mix in the sour cream and vanilla. Add the flour mixture in three batches, mixing on low speed between each addition, until you have a pliable ball of dough. Remove from the bowl and wrap in plastic. Refrigerate for at least 1 hour or up to 3 days.

While the dough is resting, make the filling: Combine the prunes, apricots, and about 3 cups water in a large saucepan. Bring to a simmer over medium heat and simmer for 10 minutes, until the fruit is plumped. Remove from the heat and let sit for 30 minutes.

Drain the fruit, reserving 1 cup of the liquid. Place the fruit in a food processor bowl or blender jar. Add the remaining 1 teaspoon cardamom and ½ cup sugar and process to make a fairly chunky filling. If it seems too thick to spread, add up to 1 cup of the cooking liquid to thin it.

Lightly flour the counter or a board. Remove the dough from the refrigerator and let it warm a little so it is easier to roll. Unwrap and cut into seven roughly equal pieces of about 9 ounces each. Set six of them aside and loosely cover them with a clean kitchen towel or plastic wrap. Roll the first piece into a rectangle 10 × 14 inches and ⅛ inch thick. Place it on a sheet of parchment paper, and using a 9 × 13-inch pan as a guide, trim the edges with a sharp knife so you have a uniform 9 × 13-inch rectangle of dough. Repeat with the remaining six pieces of dough, adding the scraps from each trimmed piece to the next. Put two or three dough rectangles, still on the parchment, on baking sheets. Stack the remaining rectangles, separated by the pieces of parchment, and refrigerate until you can bake them.

Preheat the oven to 325°F.

Place 2 or 3 baking sheets in the oven, on the upper and middle (and lower, if necessary) racks. Bake until golden and lightly brown on the edges, about 12 minutes, switching and rotating the pans after about 6 minutes for even baking. Remove from the oven and place the baked cookie layers, still on the parchment, on wire cooling racks to cool. Repeat with the remaining dough rectangles until you have baked all seven cookie layers.

To assemble, spread a thin, even layer of filling—about 1¼ cup—atop a cookie layer. Top the filling with another cookie layer. Continue until all of the cookie layers have been used. Wrap tightly in plastic and store at room temperature for at least 2 hours. It will last up to 4 days at room temperature.

After at least two hours or preferably overnight, unwrap the cake. Using a serrated knife and wiping it clean between cuts, trim the edges. The trimmed full cake should be 8 × 12 inches. The long side can be cut every 2⅜ inch to make 5 vertical rows. For each row, cut it in half, then each half cut in half, and each quarter in half to yield 8 slices per row.

Store in a covered container at room temperature, with parchment or wax paper between layers, for up to a week. Or freeze for up to a month. (The cookie layers might soften a bit, but that's okay.)

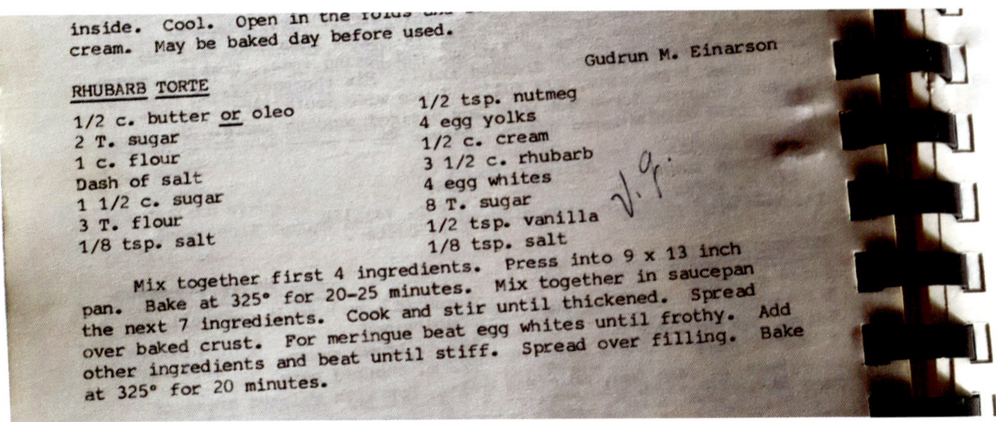

Gudrun Einarson's Rhubarb Torte

Jen Nelson, a friend and fellow local of Icelandic descent, taught me how to make her grandmother's rhubarb torte many years ago. It had been published in the *Borg Memorial Home Auxiliary Cookbook* (from the old folks' home in Mountain, the center of North Dakota's Icelandic community), a cookbook both of us inherited from our grandmothers. In my copy, Grandma Effie had noted "v.g." (for "very good") in the margin. She was right—with its buttery crust, rhubarb custard, and meringue top, it is perfect for any celebration.

Serves up to 12, depending on how you cut it

Crust

2 tablespoons granulated sugar

1 cup all-purpose flour

¼ teaspoon kosher salt (any brand)

8 tablespoons (1 stick) unsalted butter, cool but not cold, cut into chunks

To measure flour accurately by volume, scoop the flour into the measuring cup and level with a knife or other flat utensil.

Preheat the oven to 350°F. Line a 9 × 13-inch baking pan with parchment paper.

Using a pastry blender or food processor, combine the sugar, flour, and salt. Add the butter chunks and blend or process until the texture is that of coarse meal. Press into an even layer on the bottom of the prepared pan. Place the pan on the middle rack in the oven and bake for about 20 minutes, until golden, rotating the pan after 10 minutes for even baking. Remove from the oven, but leave the oven on.

Filling

1½ cups granulated sugar

3 tablespoons all-purpose flour

⅛ teaspoon kosher salt (any brand)

½ teaspoon ground or freshly grated nutmeg

4 large egg yolks*

½ cup heavy cream

3½ cups chopped rhubarb, in 1-inch pieces

Save the egg whites for the meringue below.

While the crust is baking, whisk together the sugar, flour, salt, nutmeg, egg yolks, and cream in a large, heavy-bottomed saucepan. Stir in the rhubarb. Cook over medium-low heat, stirring often, until thickened but not boiling, 5 to 7 minutes. Spread the filling over the baked crust.

Meringue Topping

4 large egg whites

½ cup granulated sugar

½ teaspoon vanilla extract

⅛ teaspoon Diamond Crystal kosher salt
  or a large pinch of other kosher salt

Place the egg whites in the bowl of a stand mixer fitted with the whisk attachment, and beat on high speed until frothy. Add the salt and beat to soft peaks. Continue to beat while adding the sugar in a gradual stream until the mixture is opaque white, and a peak of meringue will stand up when you lift the whisk. Add the vanilla and mix in completely. Spread ovenly over the filling, all the way to the edges.

To make the meringue without a stand mixer, you can use a rotary beater and beater jar or bowl, or a handheld mixer with a beater attachment.

Bake the torte for another 20 minutes, until the meringue is golden brown at the edges and set. Remove from the oven and let cool to room temperature before cutting and serving.

This can sit at room temperature, loosely covered for a half day. It can be refrigerated for up to 4 days but the meringue will weep a bit.

BERNBAUM'S
402

ESTABLISHED 2011
MADE FRESH IN
FARGO, NORTH DAKOTA
· DOCTOR BOP'S ·
FLAXSEED
CRACKERS
NET WT 4 OZ. (112 g)
CLASSIC FLAVOR
WWW.DOCTORBOPS.COM

BERNBAUM'S
PICK UP
CARRY OUT
BERNBAUM'S
DINE IN
ORDER HERE
SMOKED FISH
MOCK KRAB SALAD

Favorite BernBaum's Suppliers

Adam Ost Lamb
A small family farm in Ashley, North Dakota, that supplied us with whole lambs for many years. They don't have an online presence, but they deserve a shout-out for keeping us in Nordic Lamb Sandwiches for so long.

Doubting Thomas Farms
doubtingthomasfarms.com
Certified organic farm growing wheat, oats, millet, rye, and other heirloom grains. Fronted by the unstoppable Noreen Thomas, this farm has been on the forefront of organic production in the area for decades. We used their high-protein golden white wheat flour, rye, oats, and anything Noreen chose to bring our way (which ended up being a lot of amazing and sometimes rare products).

Earth to Jar Botanicals
facebook.com/earthtojar/
Morgan Christl has been growing beautiful herbs and microgreens for more than a decade.

Hebel & Co. Halva
hebelco.com
Delicious and organic, made in Los Angeles.

Manischewitz
manischewitz.com
This is where we procured our 50-pound bags of matzo meal (and some of their great merch).

Mandt Market
mandt-market.com
Family-run hydroponic farm in Grafton, North Dakota, with lovely greens and herbs.

Meadowlark Gardens
facebook/meadowlarkgardens/
Hydroponic tomatoes and microgreens from Park River, North Dakota.

Morey's Seafood Market
moreysmarket.com
Wonderful source for smoked fish and herring. My family loves visiting the stores whenever we are near Brainerd, Minnesota. They ship and sell nationally.

Northern Waters Smokehaus
northernwaterssmokehaus.com
Great purveyor and sandwich shop in Duluth, Minnesota. We recommend a visit, but you can order smoked fish and meat online for nationwide delivery.

Nourished by Nature
nourishedbynature.us
Bismarck, North Dakota–based regenerative ranchers Paul and Jaz Brown offer high-quality grass-fed and finished beef and lamb, pastured pork, turkey, and chicken, free-range eggs, honey, maple syrup, and other snacks—and they ship to the Lower 48.

Red River Harvest Cooperative
redriverharvest.com
A way to pick up lots of locally produced items in one place! We bought eggs and potatoes regularly.

Redhead Creamery
redheadcreamery.com
Award-winning, amazing cheeses made a few hours east of Fargo and available through their website and select markets.

The Matzo Project
matzoproject.com
For all of your matzo needs, their crackers and matzo meal are tasty, a rarity for the genre.

Underground Meats
undergroundmeats.com
Not so Jewish or Nordic, but delectable charcuterie from Madison, Wisconsin, that we sold retail and used in-house at BernBaum's.

Acknowledgments

It's hard to know where to start or end with thanks—such is the charmed life I have led.

Thank you to all of my families: the one I was born into, the one I married into, the one I helped create, my chosen family, and my friends.

This project would not have begun without my sisters being the amazing and distinctly talented people that they are. Without Jessica Baumgardner and her crack editing, re-writing, and sense of humor, this cookbook would be a pile of nonsense. Jennifer (also a great writer, editor, and wit) published the book through her Dottir Press. My sisters and I are especially grateful and lucky to be the three dottirs of Cynthia and David Baumgardner. They are loving and supportive role models as well as the best cheerleaders for our projects.

BernBaum's wouldn't have photos without the art and heart of Sarah Strong. Ali Burke created the charming watercolor illustrations, and graced BernBaum's with many visits, a very cute child in tow (double thanks for that). Thank you to Drew Stevens for bringing the book to life. Suzanne Fass did the heavy lifting of copy editing and organizing a cook's (not a writer's) book. Big gratitude to Sigrid Eyal (niece extraordinaire) for creating the index and to Billie Smith-Haffener for the thorough proofread.

Thank you to the community of local testers who must be wondering what I've been doing for the past three years.

So many talented folk added to BernBaum's (and our lives) over the years. A special thanks goes to the crew who helped us renovate our Broadway space and the menu for a "real" restaurant. It is going above and beyond to help sand and seal old wood floors, and to scrape seventy years of gunk off of a place.

I'm grateful to all the people who put care and love into BernBaum's by working there, alongside us (as with our local vendors and products), and, of course, eating at the restaurant. It was an immense gift and privilege to feed you.

Index

DON'T
LET THE
BASTARDS
GRIND YOU
DOWN

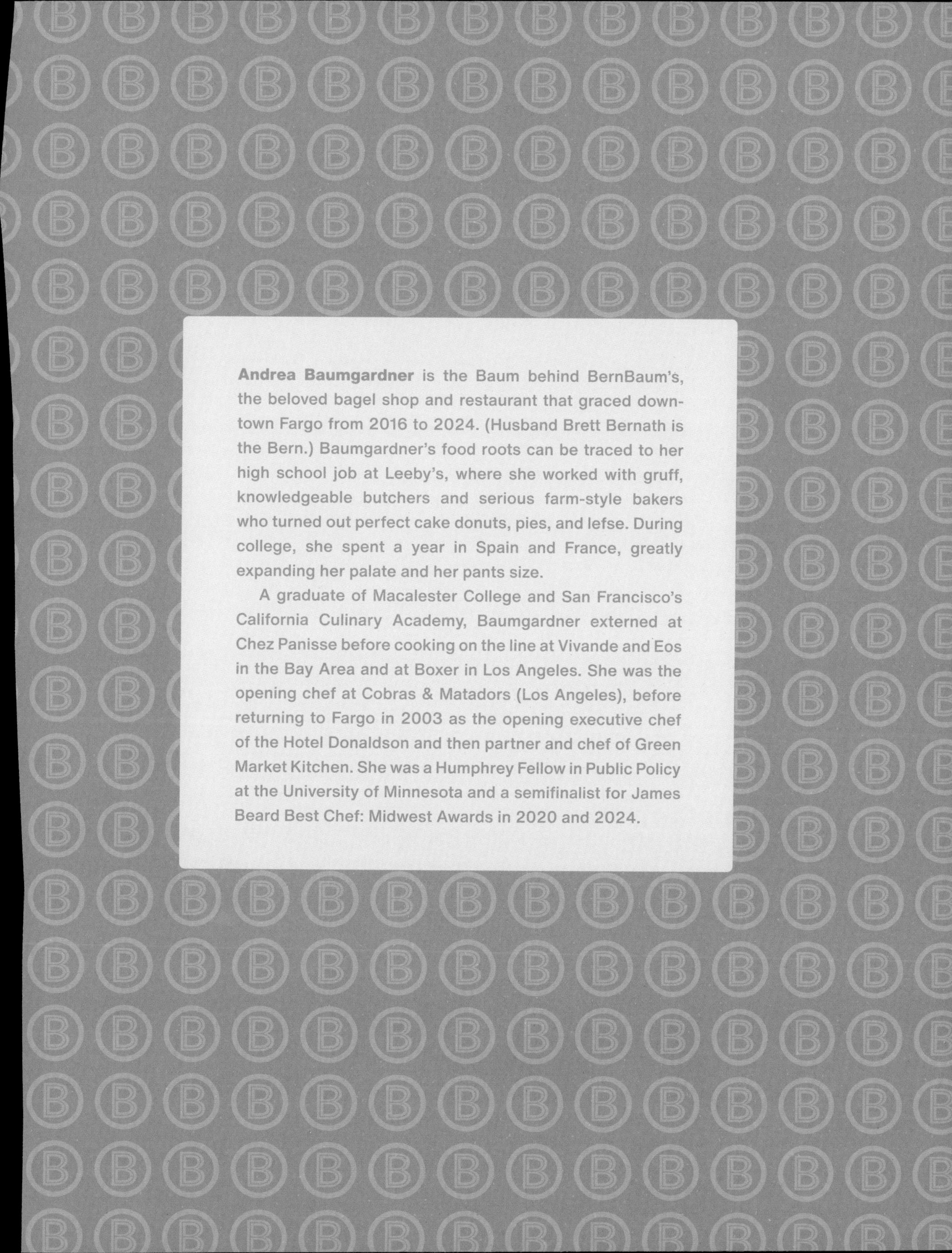

Andrea Baumgardner is the Baum behind BernBaum's, the beloved bagel shop and restaurant that graced downtown Fargo from 2016 to 2024. (Husband Brett Bernath is the Bern.) Baumgardner's food roots can be traced to her high school job at Leeby's, where she worked with gruff, knowledgeable butchers and serious farm-style bakers who turned out perfect cake donuts, pies, and lefse. During college, she spent a year in Spain and France, greatly expanding her palate and her pants size.

A graduate of Macalester College and San Francisco's California Culinary Academy, Baumgardner externed at Chez Panisse before cooking on the line at Vivande and Eos in the Bay Area and at Boxer in Los Angeles. She was the opening chef at Cobras & Matadors (Los Angeles), before returning to Fargo in 2003 as the opening executive chef of the Hotel Donaldson and then partner and chef of Green Market Kitchen. She was a Humphrey Fellow in Public Policy at the University of Minnesota and a semifinalist for James Beard Best Chef: Midwest Awards in 2020 and 2024.

♡ Kylie & Nishi

for Lovely Stephanie
to buy bagels & other tasty treats.
(You do not deserve them!)

WONDERFUL BAGELS @ BERNBAUM'S WITH MY BEAUTIFUL JULIE — WOOD PLATES, METAL FORKS FALL OFF THE — TIME TO PUT ON THE OVEN... CRISPY CHICKEN SKIN.

4/1

To Andrea & Brett — Can food feed my family — can give so good to canned meals — so yummy and for — in appreciation
ANDREA + BRETT

I LOVE COFFEE ETC AT BERNBAUM'S

I Hope that I get Bagels Evry Day!

This was the LK4H breakfast parents

"WE MUST ACCEPT FINITE DISAPPOINTMENT, BUT NEVER LOSE INFINITE HOPE."
MARTIN LUTHER KING JR.

We thought you might need this today.
All our love — Jessica
JOSIE

I'M FROM CINCINNATI, OHIO
I'M FROM RED WING, MINNESOTA

Confession — I dip popcorn in...

Afternoon by EE Cummings

dear Stranger,
I HOPE YOU ARE HAVING THE BESTEST DAY!
I WISH YOU SUNNY